Oracle of Compassion

Oracle of Compassion: The Living Word of Kuan Yin

Hope Bradford
Copyright © 2010 by Hope Bradford

All rights reserved. No part of this book may be used or reproduced in any manner whatsoever without prior written permission from the publisher, except where permitted by law.

The content of this book is intended to be general only and not as any form of advice, diagnosis or therapy and is not intended to replace competent professional advice, diagnosis or therapy. If expert assistance or counseling is needed, services of a competent professional should be sought. The content of this book (including any techniques or practices) is intended to be used as an adjunct to a rational and responsible healthcare program prescribed by a healthcare practitioner and also is intended to be used only in safe and comfortable circumstances. The Author and Publisher assume no responsibility or liability whatsoever and specifically disclaim any warranty, express or implied, for any content, techniques and/or practices or for any error or omission herein. Any use, misuse or interpretation of this book is the Purchaser's and/or Reader's sole responsibility and risk. Any perceived slight of specific people or organizations is unintentional. Any client's name and/or identity has been altered to protect their anonymity. This disclaimer applies to all content, publications, editions, modifications and articles (in all formats) featuring Hope Bradford's content and commentary and/or Lena Lees' commentary and channeled content.

This revised edition represents the preponderance of Lena Lees' original channeling of Eastern deity of compassion Kuan Yin's spiritual teachings. With theoretical commentary by Hope Bradford.

Copyright © 2010 Hope Bradford
All rights reserved.
ISBN: 1-4392-2506-0
ISBN-13: 9781439225066

Library of Congress Control Number: 2009900270

Visit www.booksurge.com to order additional copies.

HOPE BRADFORD

ORACLE OF COMPASSION
THE LIVING WORD OF KUAN YIN

2010

Oracle of Compassion

TABLE OF CONTENTS

Introduction xix
a personal channel • singular psychic event • spiritual canons • Kuan Yin as shape-shifter • Water Moon Goddess • spirit world • an affinity with the Goddess Kuan Yin

Chapter One 1
Auspicious Dreams & Paintings
Thinking and emotions make it so • human consciousness • client-centered hypnosis • spectrum of consciousness • visionary painting • dream of being baptized • conch shell & the Buddhist eight auspicious symbols • right speech • liquid that reminds people of their oneness • keep your spirit connection

Chapter Two 9
My Intention to Meet Kuan Yin Created Her
Guides, visionaries & healers • Kuan Yin: energy manifested into form • intention • karmic connection • karmic path • tarot cards • no wrong choice • life lesson: simplicity • commentary: one's point of intention is one's attraction point

Chapter Three 13
Lifetimes to Tell
learning compassion and determination • compassion for the masses • hurt which can propel someone in a positive direction • children and humanity • life: one image in an entire role of film • the *other side* is vital to living • old teachings & beliefs • commentary: the symbiotic relationship between intention and attention

Chapter Four 17
"I Know the Whole Story"
personal choices • different saints and demigods • varying stages of human evolution • attaining a state of consciousness or comfort beyond one's current level • *empathy*, detached compassion • understand with your senses • develop the words to understand • earth is a very young planet • acknowledge and experience this part of the universe • karma is intricate • tools to really, truly love • love everyone as you would love your children • commentary: you have great freedom to choose

Chapter Five 23
Shrouded Kuan Yin
consciously choosing and directing karma • robe of death • mothers' love, the most powerful love in the world • humanity's resources, love and free will • earth is in a certain karmic cycle • at peace with death • helping those passing over to connect with loved ones and complete the process • Kuan Yin knows the *whole story* • grief as a potent force • Kuan Yin's healing elixir • Kuan Yin turning agony into pure love with her potion • commentary: love, free will and Kuan Yin's Law of Compassion

Chapter Six 29
"All of Life Is a Prayer"
prayer and great intention • existence is eternal • individual's 'spark' or existence • open systems • developing a potent energy • ego-based power • evil is just a label • full spectrum of humanity • one's humanity is a powerful place to be • reincarnation and repeating lessons not learned • fear of death • nothing can harm me • thinking yourself there • life perceived as a curse or punishment • pain exists because of fear • commentary: believing in one's power and Kuan Yin's Law of Compassion

Chapter Seven 35
The Breadcrumb Maker
traditional hypnosis countdown • focusing on nature • planting the spiritual "seed" • staying constant and aware in your love • consciously directed love (prayers) • acceptance of differences • limiting collective consciousness • the great divide • *the love and*

forgiveness principle • thoughts can change the course of history • karmic acceleration • winds of these times • one's true divine and peaceful nature • voices of the divine spirit • commentary: catching the wind

Chapter Eight 41
"The Universe Will Bring People Anything They Want"
mind expanding teachings • gravitation of similar vibration thought structures • unsnarling the beliefs entangling humanity • *compassion for the untruth* • *Law of the Liberation (Spiritualization) of Matter* • Evolutionary Potentials (probable realities) • karma as "made up stories" • concepts and images • worldview • Kuan Yin's 21 Law of Compassion precepts

Chapter Nine 47
Loving Kindness
the world is about the different stages people are in • amplified senses • reincarnational patterns • spirit energies • soul evolution • suffering state of mind • demigods waiting in line to be born • evolving from a different *angle* • clashes between *energies* are a result of a "better than" mindset • eternal beings • reality is always truth, knowledge and bliss • addiction to negative news • reality as a microcosm of the whole • blast into a ball of light • karmic *fog* • teach my message, practice my message • commentary: more love, more joy!

Chapter Ten 53
Kuan Yin with a Thousand-Arms
human mistakes and inaccuracies are no less important than divinity • acknowledge and extract divinity from one's trials and tribulations • divine part of self • plants have enormous intelligences and spirituality • environmental destruction • conditional love • death is like giving birth • falling in love with a new life • mind to mind understanding • examples in nature of how to behave, live in harmony • tools humans can use to balance their lives • eternal connection • commentary: remember to marvel!

Chapter Eleven 59
The Good and Pious Warriors

heightened senses • planet of origin • movement through the earth plane • attaining spiritual completeness • loving god • karmic connection & path • oneness, the point of no identity • embrace humanity • geographical power centers • collective agreement • collective energy • commentary: a vision of sustainable technology on earth

Chapter Twelve 65
The Most Divine Life Imaginable

Buddha and Kuan Yin are like brother and sister • Kuan Yin appears in many forms constructed from people's perceptions • Kuan Yin will be here until the last soul passes over • path of liberation • no two paths look the same • realistic life and motherhood • commentary: utilizing imagination and creativity to solve a challenging situation

Chapter Thirteen 71
Living the Dream

see my image, create my image • understand all my manifestations and watch my pastimes • Kuan Yin knows the whole story and it's already over • juggling the dream and the world of dreams • Kuan Yin and Buddha carved deeply in the rocks • earth is reflective of the different kinds of evolution • commentary: evolutionary potentials and personal resonance: the power of free will

Chapter Fourteen 77
Dragon-Riding Kuan Yin

Creation of expansive or entrapping realities • global investment • out-of-body energies • "untruth" has magnified itself • a giant disk of great density • thoughts make up this disk • energy of 'good' • three primary limiting beliefs: "survival of the fittest", "not enough" and "better than" • alchemy • compassion for the "untruth" • sparks of light • great mix of free will and karma • dynamics of the universe • commentary: collective agreements, invested identities and Kuan Yin's Law of Compassion

Chapter Fifteen 85
Touching the Tree
the present as a *vehicle* for attracting reality • thoughts can influence world affairs • valuing children as teachers • creating possibilities • place of extreme sensitivity was carved in your soul • empathy & loving-kindness are different from guilt or pity • true empathy is understanding pain and suffering from a place of power • commentary: visualizing anything

Chapter Sixteen 91
The Divinity of Humanity
path to peace • made-up realities • being present means an absence of past and future • bringing the mind into the present is the link to eternity • moments to be lived • life is the dream • authenticate your life • collective agreement • living on both planes of reality and making it work • philosophy behind meditation • commentary: rendering an ordinary drama, spiritual: the power of the word

Chapter Seventeen 97
Divine Realms
filter of fear • realms where there is no fear • in such [divine] realms realization is complete • on earth there often does not exist a feeling of oneness • nothing can harm or destroy you • fear comes from not knowing the entire truth • a second of thought about Kuan Yin is very potent • difficult times and spiritual growth • commentary: choosing love over fear

Chapter Eighteen 103
One's Core Being—Pure Soul Essence
clean and clear wealth of higher consciousness • simultaneously aware • alternate reality • beings in this dimension desire higher consciousness • poverty consciousness • reasons for suffering are personal and varied • pure soul essence • karmic element of self which agrees to suffering • core being • rapid-fire visuals of flowers and plants • commentary: the inner light: my dream of core (soul) essence

Chapter Nineteen 109
The Power of Good Intention
inner core, karmic debt • magical power that is part of the Authentic Self • disconnected or misaligned chakras • "stomach area of life" • mothering element in our society • layers one takes to the soul • various brainwaves help us to go beyond, under the layers of karma • skin holds the spirit in place • praying for others' well-being • commentary: powerful magnetic fields of attraction

Chapter Twenty 117
Spiritual Liberation
sense of time in one world is not the same as in another • heartache, heart congestion • dusting, polishing the glass of one's own heart • lifetimes of blockages • being a "conduit" • three excellent spiritual practices • spirituality as liberating • "planetary karmic build-up" • "planetary imprint" • earth represents a certain level of learning • grand experiment • things are right on schedule • your precious earth cannot be destroyed • commentary: fear of death can create Law of Compassion setbacks

Chapter Twenty-One 123
Ask and Receive
grounded and centered • the law of karma • one's "open space" • being human is an opportunity to bring spirit into all that is material • fear can change one's original intention • ask and receive • parallel life • two polarized and entrapping lifetimes • commentary: ask and receive: goals that have been with us for lifetimes

Chapter Twenty-Two 131
"Remember the Possibilities"
possibilities of something greater than is here now • prosperity can happen at any time • the *diamond* represents consciousness, love and all other forms of non-materialistic abundance • hypnosis as a powerful tool • sound comes first in the universe • we're all made of sound • commentary: vibration tuning: developing your relationship with sound

Chapter Twenty-Three　　　　　　　　　　　　　　　137
"Remember Us in Our Beauty and Our Love"
effects of sound and vibrations upon physicality • relying upon spiritual practices • pray for others • endless possibilities • it's all about faith • utilizing your human experience by practicing meditation or visualization • the *watcher* • hypnosis and chakra alignment techniques • letting go of former beliefs and impressions • believe you are valuable, worthy • a looped tape going round and round • commentary: tonal resonance and the outward progression of consciousness

Chapter Twenty-Four　　　　　　　　　　　　　　　145
Seasons of Life
no beginning or end, only *seasons of life* • karma and decision-making • instant attraction and karma • practicing being in the moment • savoring each moment • the wind that is blowing right now • seen and unseen elements • commentary: invested elements: karma and free will

Chapter Twenty-Five　　　　　　　　　　　　　　　153
"Be Still & Watch the Spider Build Its Web"
utilizing the power of your accomplishments • clearing stagnant energy • all those existing on the earth are in this together • collective planetary intention and personal responsibility • a visualization for letting go • we only have the power to help ourselves • taking shelter in the arts • celebrating the beauty of the local culture • attraction options • mind chatter • ideas don't just float in the universe, they're linked together • commentary: the shape of manifestation

Chapter Twenty-Six　　　　　　　　　　　　　　　159
Kuan Yin & the Elephant
crystallizing the components of a lesson • belief that one doesn't have options • relationships and two frequent mistakes • *driving force* for one's life path • passion for a certain life path • mistrust can bring impoverishment • following one's heart, continuing on one's *divine path*, can bring abundance • communicating with love • commentary: emotions and Kuan Yin's Law of Compassion

Chapter Twenty-Seven   167
Many Flavors of Ice Cream
developing a greater capacity to love • you've already lived 'future lives' • death as a doorway to other realities • tasting everything • fearing disaster • desire is why you're here • the God Force likes intense pleasure • *simple-living and high-thinking* • believing in a certain reality • taking events too personally • commentary: attract only those 'flavors' you wish for your life

Chapter Twenty-Eight   177
Eight Senses
powerful meditation • reality, truth and the importance of life • two types of people • Gulf of Mexico Oil Spill • an *energy* manifested from planetary beliefs • souls "volunteered" to be at the center of this drama • karma and family relationships • reactions of *all* beings and events • there is an *energetic reaction* to something in print • power of the word • "printed word of humanity" • commentary: the wondrous opportunity

About the Author

"Sit with me in divine faith and believe in me. And I'll be there!"
-Kuan Yin

INTRODUCTION

"This is just another dimension, another manifestation of all Kuan Yin's manifestations: the goddess as a young maiden, her robe with its long flowing train. Clutching this, I follow it to where it tumbles down, disappearing into a black starry hole, a swirling darkness that takes me into the universe. Still clasping Her gown, I am riding high above the earth. I see how gossamer layers of white silken material have opened up, allowing prayers and blessings to shower the earth."
-*Lena Lees*

In these 'interesting times', Kuan Yin, Eastern deity of compassion, comes to us through the words of this manuscript with her powerful message of love and hope. Known and worshipped throughout the world, she addresses the human condition with clarity and compassion.

Having experienced psychic 'visitations' her entire life, Lena Lees then found herself (from her very first hypnosis session) conversing with Kuan Yin. Focusing upon the power of loving-kindness and how to most effectively travel one's life path, Kuan Yin speaks with immediacy and ardor. This transcription of her channeled words and spiritual precepts is unique as it represents a direct and authentic communication with this ancient goddess.

Covering issues as diverse as "the amazing mix of free will and karma" and one's personal "path of liberation" this manuscript features an informative dialogue on Kuan Yin's Law of Compassion.

Through metaphor and imagery, Kuan Yin demonstrates how we (as energies) are the attractors of reality. With infinite love and compassion, the Goddess explains these incredibly profound concepts: that there are only moments upon moments to be lived and one's beliefs and focused intent are the magnets for reality.

A Singular Psychic Event

Indeed, the story may have begun when Ms. Lees prayed to a beautiful stone visage of Kuan Yin. Having traveled from California to visit with family and friends in Philadelphia, Lena knew this would be the last time, for a while, that she'd be able to visit the East Coast. Placing a visit to the Philadelphia Museum of Art on her family's vacation itinerary, Lena had no idea of the importance of her decision, how it would later profoundly transform her life.

At the museum with her husband and children by her side, she suddenly gravitated to a room boasting an impressive display of Asian shrines and statuary. Drawn to a particularly striking sculpture of Kuan Yin, Lena believed the statue was comforting her, *speaking* to her. Beseeching Kuan Yin, she and her family asked for assistance with the many challenges they faced ahead. Several years later; making an appointment with me, Lena found herself engaged in an ongoing conversation; channeling the words and spiritual canons of the ancient Asian deity.

A librarian, student and mother of three, Lena had originally scheduled an appointment with me early in March 2004, to discuss and troubleshoot her college graduation project. Not knowing much about hypnosis, she was anxious to discover if she could go into trance.

To satisfy my Client-Centered Hypnosis internship practitioner hour requirements, I agreed to hypnotize Lena. To my amazement, I heard Lena speak, while in trance, powerful phrases and metaphor that were utterly foreign to her. Incredibly, upon waking from her trance, she remembered nothing.

Believing Lena's first encounter with the Goddess Kuan Yin was a chance one-time event, I listened attentively (but with a healthy skepticism) during our second session together. By the third episode, I knew that something remarkable had occurred.

From her first hypnosis induction, forward, Lena realized she had a personal "channel"; some mysterious and lingering association with Kuan Yin.

From the onset, it appeared Lena had a natural affinity with the Goddess. Further into this channeling phenomenon, it was revealed that Lena had worshipped Kuan Yin throughout many lifetimes, that because of their former relationship Lena's personage is imminently compatible for bearing this Goddess's compassionate message.

When transcribing the Kuan Yin material, I often wondered if She somehow knew Lena would always ask selfless questions, that because of her love for humanity, Lena also had true compassion. Indeed, to facilitate an authentic channeling of Kuan Yin's Law of Compassion theories, the once separate consciousnesses of Lena and Kuan Yin were inextricably bound during each of the sessions. Typically, Lena's trance discourse (along with masterfully interpreting Kuan Yin's unique language and ever-transforming visages) involved questions spontaneously rising up into her consciousness.

Sometimes her inquiries methodically followed the original theme of a given session. On other occasions, however, Lena's new line of questioning could initiate entire new discussion threads. Obviously, new topics spontaneously introduced by Lena were (because of this unique melding of consciousness), at least partially, influenced by Kuan Yin.

Kuan Yin's unique language styling and vast spiritual lexicon is a form of *non-linear language.* (In many world traditions, there exist classic variations on non-linear language including shamanic journeys and speaking in tongues.) Lena was confronted (at the onset of each discourse) with the challenge of navigating the sometimes-foreboding waters of out-of-time reality. In addition to deciphering Kuan Yin's non-linear verbiage, Lena would routinely describe the Deity's complex and rapidly morphing visages.

Spokespersons for the Goddess of Compassion

Highly venerated deity in the Chinese Pantheon and known by thousands throughout the ages, Kuan Yin has periodically appeared and spoken to villagers throughout the Orient. Spreading comfort and wisdom, she is the embodiment of mercy and compassion. Consecrated ground, Kuan Yin's sacred sites are considered her abodes. Because of their purity, these locations are also designated as her pilgrimage sites, places of worship.

Also known as Avalokiteshvara, Padmapani, Chenrigzi, Shadakshari, Water, Moon Goddess, and Deity with a Thousand Eyes, Kuan Yin has been worshipped at temples, pagodas and shrines throughout the world as both a male and female deity. As this deity came to Ms. Lees as primarily female, I will refer to Kuan Yin (throughout the text), as feminine in nature.

Now, appearing again, speaking through Lena, Kuan Yin offered her wondrous insight and wisdom, spirituality for our times. As the United States (at the time of these channelings), was engaged in a war with Iraq, Lena, (similar to many at the time), had myriad urgent questions. Most importantly, she yearned to know how the world could become more peaceful.

Discovering from Kuan Yin that the earth is in a particular "karmic cycle", Lena wanted to understand more about Her perspective on the nature of this historical era. Lena also had many questions concerning the nature of one's personal path. This often triggered long and intricate exchanges about how we as citizens of the earth can better comprehend and appreciate our human condition. Listening to Kuan Yin, it became apparent that beliefs and global events are intimately linked.

Often, the session formats manifested as intense questions and answers between Lena and Kuan Yin. Impressed by Lena's ability to precisely detail her and Kuan Yin's deeply spiritual and thought-provoking dialogue, I could only marvel. Indeed, Kuan Yin concedes: *"it is difficult for some to hear the voices of the Divine Spirit"*. Lena's verbal adroitness renders Kuan Yin's often-challenging precepts approachable for the common reader. Possessing an uncanny ability for relaying complex phrases and concepts of not only Kuan Yin, but those who no longer dwell in the physical world, Lena accurately relayed discussions with other spirits who could, quite unexpectedly, voice their opinions.

Panoply of the Senses

Through the years of teaching and facilitating hypnosis, I was aware that when one goes into trance (alpha brainwave rhythms) or dreams (theta brainwave rhythms), one enters a *non-linear* world void of time, space parameters. Because of their contrast to the waking (beta) self, non-linear realms can be problematic when trying to accurately translate and relay information from "alpha" to "beta" reality.

Similar to a computer having to, for example, reformat files so to conform to newer programming versions, the psychic channel is presented with the task of accurately 'formatting' non-linear verbiage and images into a linear format.

Feeling Kuan Yin's energy flowing through her, Lena was able to assume Kuan Yin's mercurial persona. Articulating Kuan Yin's concepts, Lena could describe her garb and backdrops as if she was there.

Such a transcendent process might be compared to a child relaying her/his ecstatic feelings when frolicking in some forth or fifth dimensional garden. Overwhelmed by the immediacy and sensuality of its beauty, the child is fully engaged, utilizing a multiplicity of senses. Unlike Lena, however, the child may not yet have the words to convey the full multidimensionality of their experience.

Sometimes Lena would need to pause, telling me, *"I'm just going to sit with Kuan Yin, for a moment, and try to comprehend what she is telling me. It is primarily images and metaphor that I must form into whole sentences. Sometimes I don't understand how I am able to speak full phrases and thoughts set forth by Her."*

Lena once described the process involved in selecting the perfect words to convey Kuan Yin's often-complex concepts and sentences similar to "a stick floating down a stream". Confessing that sometimes the entire process could be quite challenging, Lena went on to explain:

"That very same 'stick', which usually floated so effortlessly down the stream, could get hung up on a rock or on the shore. I'd know, then that the alignment was wrong. As a consequence, I would have a bad taste or a similar sensation signaling that things weren't quite right, that I needed to refine my interpretation. All along, I was aware that I was no different from anyone else. Kuan Yin constantly reminded me that I was not special, but that she has deeply valued meeting with me throughout these weeks and months. She told me she hoped I would always come to her for comfort and guidance. Kuan Yin also mentioned that her information wasn't just limited to my interpretations; that passing concepts and truth through different beings results in various perceptions and interpretations."

***

Because she rarely recalled what was said during her altered state, Lena would often have to review afterward, for her own clarification. Interestingly, seasoned channels do not necessarily bring forth information conforming to their own personal worldview. In fact, there are numerous examples demonstrating that channeled information may even represent an opposing view.

There seemed another, inexplicable element at work. Although Lena attempted several times to channel Kuan Yin on her own, her extraordinary abilities primarily occurred when I was present in the room. During a memorable passage, the Goddess mentioned that not only was her energy congruent with Lena's, but she also enjoyed a special connection with me. Indeed, I often experienced dreams featuring specific directives for the book from Kuan Yin.

Lena and I both came to believe the process was more complicated then we originally assumed; that my energy somehow served as a *psychic fulcrum* assisting Lena in bringing forth the Kuan Yin material. Often, while Kuan Yin was responding to my questions, Lena would observe the Goddess moving closer and embracing me: *"She's right by you. She has her arms around you, Hope. Kuan Yin wants you to know that she loves and counts on you so much."*

Approaching the time of the actual layout and production of the book, I was haunted by a series of dreams in which a pregnant woman was the main character. On the verge of birthing, she came to me nightly for almost a week. While I couldn't be certain, I always suspected this mysterious woman was Kuan Yin, foretelling the completion of the manuscript.

Later, I dreamt of giving birth to a beautiful babe swathed in white silken brocade. Abandoning the infant's side for but a moment, I was shocked to discover an empty cradle upon my return.

Awakened by my own sheer terror, I realized that this dream was only a metaphor: The challenging, inspirational process of chronicling Kuan Yin's message and pastimes was now complete. Moving through Lena and me like air being breathed in and then out again, the Kuan Yin's teachings could now be released to the world.

Unexpected Encounters

Well into the writing of the Kuan Yin material, another curious event occurred. Inviting a close friend, Susan, over to see my remodeled dining room, I was delighted to visit with her once again. Showing her a Kuan Yin painting I'd just completed, we sat on the couch, having tea and visiting together. It had been a while since we'd seen each other, so we had a lot of catching up to do.

Preparing to leave, Susan pointed excitedly towards the dining-room window, exclaiming: *"Look! Just beyond the window! I see Kuan Yin! She is telling me you're to construct a grotto with a painting of her inside, right out there in the garden."*

Then regarding me intently, Susan asked, *"Are there really such things? I mean stone grottos containing paintings or sculptures of Kuan Yin?"*

"Oh yes," I replied. *"They're quite common in the East. There are roadside grottos where people come to worship and pray to the Goddess."*

"I know it's really Kuan Yin because I'm seeing Her many arms," relayed Susan, excitedly.

"Can you see? The hair is standing up on my arms. That's how I know this is happening to me; that what I'm witnessing is really true."

"I wish I could see her now and share in your vision," I replied, peering in the direction that Susan had been pointing. *"I know, however, she has been a constant presence throughout the creation of this manuscript. Consoling, encouraging, her energy has been a great comfort throughout the entire process."*

***

Over the months and years of our friendship, I've gradually learned more about Lena Lees' extraordinary life: the events preceding that fateful encounter with Kuan Yin in the museum. As a child, Ms. Lee's natural inclination was to talk to the trees. They were her friends. During the challenging times, she found solace in the shade of a particularly beautiful Eastern Maple near her home.

Knowing in her heart, that they were sentient beings, she once even insisted her mother place a band aide on the bark of a tree she had accidentally bumped into while riding her tricycle. Having such a close bond with trees, it is therefore not surprising that during one of her psychic transmissions, she found herself sitting with Kuan Yin atop the wide canopy of that exquisite Eastern Maple.

Experiencing soul visitations while sound asleep, Lena (from early childhood) began to comprehend that she had special abilities. Imploring her assistance, these souls were constantly drawn to Lena. The reason for their cosmic sojourn was simple. They had recently passed over and needed her to reassure and console their relatives. Lena's clairvoyant gift of speaking to and comforting newly passed souls persisted.

It was primarily Kuan Yin and Lena conversing with each other, during most of the channeled passages. However, previously unknown 'voices', personas from the spirit world, would occasionally intervene, actively participating in the discourse. Was Lena's special ability to hear these departed souls, now affording her a predisposition towards mediumship? I do not pretend to know the answer.

By adolescence, this nightly phenomenon was a motivation for seeking spiritual answers. As a young adult deeply involved in her spiritual studies, Lena once stole into the main prayer hall of the meditation center for morning asana. Quieting her mind, sitting calmly in meditative pose, her serenity was suddenly pierced by a loud blast. Startled, leaping up, she saw large glass shards: millions of bits of broken glass strewn across the floor.

Confusion and then relief! Realizing she was unharmed, she saw others streaming into the main hall. Still mesmerized before the utterly shattered plate-glass window, Lena couldn't help but wonder what sign this might be from the universe. What did this spectacular event bode for the future?

The Crown Jewel of Compassion

A profusion of shapes, Kuan Yin draws upon her vast repertoire of archetypes demonstrating the plasticity of the soul. Beautiful young maiden, mother or wizened crone! Death and rebirth! Undulating rock formations and fathomless galaxies! These are but samplings of her clever and boundless transformational powers. What Kuan Yin is attempting through her mind-expanding teachings and metamorphisms is to show how to put the pieces together into the meaningful mosaic that is our *Authentic Self*.

Almost always encountered near bamboo, water and beautiful rock formations, during the weekly hypnosis sessions, Kuan Yin effortlessly *becomes* her surroundings. Kuan Yin's Law of Compassion is the most powerful form of the universal like attract like magnetizing force. It can therefore bring to one "the most divine life imaginable": all that is good.

Throughout the sessions, I became aware of certain consistent themes. Along with her emphasis concerning the attraction powers of beliefs and vibrations was Kuan Yin's *Love and Forgiveness Principle*. Her flamboyant personality and style opened important new Law of Compassion vistas.

Perhaps the most important decision one can make in his or her life is whether one possesses absolute self-determinism; whether one's thoughts do indeed attract reality. Indeed, Buddha has stated: *"All that we are is the result of what we have thought. The mind is everything. What we think, we become."*

Yet, if there is any doubt that we control our destiny, there may be hesitation in all we say and do. People sometimes wish for miracles, not realizing the miracle of the body, mind and spirit synergy that supports self-determinism.

This work codifies the centrality of free will, humanity's primary resources of love and compassion, the primacy of sound and frequency and humanity's collective agreement concerning the three main detrimental beliefs: "better than", "not enough" and "survival of the fittest". Humanity's potential to attract the most beneficial reality by imagining the possibilities and Kuan Yin's *Love and Forgiveness Principle* will also be discussed in depth.

Now, I have little doubt that it was Lena's and my quests for truth that attracted Kuan Yin's attention. A tapestry of found pieces to the cosmic puzzle coupled with astounding phenomenon, what follows is an account of a spiritual sojourn involving Lena and her Muse. A sentence by sentence chronicling of how through hypnosis, Asia's ancient Deity, Kuan Yin spoke through spiritual channel, Lena Lees, this work demonstrates how we hold within us the twin potentials for self-determinism: free will and compassion.

Kuan Yin has decreed: "I'm here for you eternally." So now, allow yourself to be taken on a journey into Kuan Yin's world. It is a place of lush bamboo forests, mystical waterfalls and rock formations and all nature of flora and fauna, even stars and galaxies! It is also a place of profound spiritual insights and metaphor. *"Fall into the water!"*

1
Auspicious Dreams & Paintings

"You create your whole world from your thoughts. Say and believe that you can have the most divine life imaginable. Believe and be open to receiving."
-Kuan Yin

Several years ago, before I knew Lena, I dreamt of meeting a fair-haired woman in a parallel universe. Adjacent to one another in some ephemeral classroom we watched idly as people milled about, talking. We suddenly focused on one another, standing across rows of student's desks. Awkwardly, we waited for the other to speak.

Finally, I said, "I wonder what's going on; where are we?"

Following my rather audacious inquiry, there was a long silence, what seemed like an eternity. Statue-like, the woman did not respond.

Overcome by myriad doubts and even more questions, I held my breath. Had I been too forward? Would she walk away? Was this woman, indeed, friend or foe?

Quite innocently the woman finally replied, "I wonder too!"

Instantaneously, as if two wires had made contact, a powerful current coursed through my body. Awakened to this mind-to-mind connection, trust and then love welled up from my dormant heart. Pulsating through my body, what had been doubt and fear changed into waves of friendship and love. Simultaneously, the strong, positive emotions were altered into pure thought. In some inexplicable mind-body synergy, thoughts melted into words, swiftly undulating up through my solar plexus, heart and throat. Rolling forward and off my tongue was a convergence of sound, my own unique tonalities.

Navigating through a warehouse overflowing with Greek and Roman statuary, the woman and I then ascended a long, spiral staircase. Finally stepping upon a mezzanine where an orchestra prepared for its debut, the discordant sounds of the musicians tuning their instruments temporarily shook me from my reverie. Listening intently, somehow hearing above the loud cacophony, I sensed an invisible stream of energy; a gentle unity transcending the dissonance.

Approaching the podium, the conductor readied himself, leafing open his musical score and raising his baton. Transfixed, the musicians then lifted their instruments in unison.

Commencing with a violin solo, the wistful strains of the string section lilted towards the starry heavens. Joining in, three flautists harmonized with the bassoon as it droned a somber adagio. Merging with the short staccato rhythms of the piano, the violins initiated their building crescendo after which the horn section trumpeted its finale. Replacing the baton, the conductor turned and bowed.

Turning their heads almost in unison; placing their instruments on the floor beside their chairs, the musicians watched as my friend and I showered hundreds of white roses upon the audience below.

Awake; amazed and delighted at my own lightening-quick mind/body connection, I was (at that moment) exquisitely aware of how thinking and emotions make it so—how we are the creators of our universe. Only partially awake, there was still something I didn't quite understand. Having felt the infinite vitality of the universe coursing through my body, I understood the powerful sequence of my personal mind/body events emerging from that mind-to-mind contact. While these initially appeared to be random, disconnected occurrences, I came to understand that the entire process was one integral event.

Additionally, while I didn't comprehend the full implications of my meeting the golden-haired woman, I knew that on some significant level she and I had connected. To this day, the profound feelings of oneness still haunt me.

Reflecting upon the dream now, I realize she bore a striking resemblance to Lena. So it was; that when I finally met her in waking reality, she seemed strangely familiar to me.

I wonder about occurrences of this nature: instances where people seem to already know each other. For example when someone, during a casual conversation comments: *"You look so familiar to me. Have we met before?"* Even more inexplicable is when two people, who've never met, experience romantic feelings. Is it karmic? Or is it because these individuals have already met in dreams?

Delving Into the Spectrum of Consciousness

During the fall of 2003, I was involved in studying the (at least) five human brainwave periodicities. Initially, the information I was in the process of gathering was intended for use in a final project for my Client-Centered Hypnosis class.

A counselor and artist for over twenty years, I strived to learn as much as I could about what I termed the human "spectrum of consciousness". Possessing a deep curiosity concerning the various and specific complex human behaviors and interactions occurring within the five-brainwave frequency ranges, I was especially intrigued by the trance (alpha), dream (theta) and gamma (ultra high frequency) ranges.

During this same period of my life, I also began another project, a portrait. As an artist, I sometimes get *called*, inspired by some muse to create a spirit painting, to depict visages or people not of this world. This genre of painting is sometimes referred to as visionary painting. Feeling some urgency, the spirit energy channeling through me, I quickly set brush to canvas.

Erudite features: elaborate, bejeweled headdress atop her dark, swept-back hair, I could only conclude she was descended of Chinese royalty. Working feverishly, I never completed my vision. Unfortunately, with the hypnosis class consuming all my time and energy, I was compelled to put the painting on the back burner. Returning to the canvas over a year later, I recognized exactly who this woman was.

During this same period of my life, I experienced two auspicious dreams. In the first, I was a baby crying idly in my crib. Suddenly soothed by the rhythmic flapping of wings, I ceased my futile wailing: *"You see?"* explained a voice from the ethers, *"Even as a baby, you perceived and were comforted by the higher frequency resonance. You intuitively knew it was the source of all reality just as you intuitively understood you were safe."*

Later, in that very dream, I experienced myself as an adult standing in an auditorium. To my amazement, I was being honored in a ceremony. Reverently, a young boy placed a conch shell at my feet. Awake and perplexed, I pondered the significance of the conch shell. Not too familiar with Buddhist precepts, I was told by a friend that such a shell most likely represents *right speech*. I wondered later if the dream depicted a degree of intuitive maturity: right speech that would greatly assist me in interpreting the Kuan Yin material's more complex passages. Certain ancient texts also describe the conch shell as symbolic for calling forth the Gods and Goddesses.

Soon after, another dream also portended the coming of a greatly honored personage or work:

Venturing out into the darkness, I found myself at the edge of a small harbor. Drawn by the plaintive calls of the moored boats, I watched as some ancient wind taunted the lashed sails. One craft in particular seized my attention.

Completely entranced, I realized it bore a great resemblance to an oil painting I'd abandoned on the shore. Gingerly, I stepped onto a single wooden plank, the only apparent route to the boat. Edging forward, I couldn't know whether this narrow beam was a real dock or just flotsam on the water. Nearing its end, my bodyweight suddenly overwhelmed the flimsy and treacherous board, submerging it, and me along with it.

Then, I felt my body go deep beneath the waves. Gasping, I eventually shot out of the dark waters, back into waking reality.

"Fall into the water," Kuan Yin had once instructed, referring to the *waters of consciousness*. In retrospect, I'm certain that these dreams were preludes to Kuan Yin's imminent arrival: what would eventually be my own *sounding* of the depths of consciousness.

An Auspicious Meeting

Prior to embarking upon client-centered Hypnosis, I had an abiding interest in Kuan Yin's Law of Compassion. I wanted to further understand the role of beliefs, intention and emotional patterns in waking reality as well as in reincarnational patterns.

Still engaged in my research, I focused upon the importance of belief and intention: their influence upon even events occurring in the alternative brainwave periodicities. I was fascinated to learn, while cramming for my hypnosis certification that newer hypnosis philosophies; specifically Client-Centered Hypnosis, techniques teach that a client's intention and trance-goal help to determine the structure and focus of each hypnotic experience. The clear difference is that traditional hypnotic inductions mostly utilize standardized scripts usually not requiring client-input.

Conversely, Client-Centered hypnosis primarily provides a customized script based entirely upon the individual client's issues, goals and even phraseology. This is established during the all-important intake period and is a crucial first step in setting the stage for one's inner work. During the hypnosis countdown and actual trance experience the hypnotist will utilize this input to help personalize and create a familiarity that the client can identify with. Further, one's intention combined with specific phraseology has the potential to *activate* specific and relevant memories.

Having experienced this process, personally, I understand the power of intention and words, how they can greatly assist in accessing profound meaning and answers for one's life. Client-centered hypnosis techniques, I am certain were instrumental in helping my client, Lena Lees; achieve her deep trance-level.

Once a client reaches a satisfactory level of trance, there is an opportunity for problem solving; such as learning how to be calm, build self-esteem, alter unhelpful habits through positive imagery, etc. or to process whatever issue is currently presenting itself.

In February of 2004, I invited an acquaintance, Lena Lees, to experience this client-centered approach to hypnosis. I explained that I had several years of prior therapy experience and that I was still immersed in my client-centered studies. I told Lena her session with me would fulfill my weekly homework requirement. Describing the process, I also delineated another countdown technique our class was presently focused upon called *transpersonal hypnosis*. Informing Lena that she had the option of either a traditional or transpersonal countdown, we set the appointment date.

Transpersonal hypnosis employs a ten to zero countdown similar to a traditional countdown protocol. Once, however, one has established her/his *safe place*, (a potential fallback, resource position if, for any reason, one feels unsafe during trance), she/he is directed to their *sacred place*. One's *sacred place* is whatever the client experiences, once the directive is made. *Sacred places* vary greatly from one individual to the next but very often represent one's deepest sense of the divine.

Agreeing to meet with me for her first trance induction, Lena mentioned during our phone intake together, that her goal for her first trance experience was to receive guidance on how to refine her college graduation thesis, to get a better idea of how her final project would take shape:

Utilizing the client-centered approach, I conducted the standard interview, completing a custom intake sheet for Lena. Understanding that she had initially come to trouble-shoot the particulars for her college field study project, I explained that my homework project had to do specifically with transpersonal hypnosis. Detailing further, I relayed that even a very pragmatic question, such as hers, could still be addressed in one's potentially more spiritual, transpersonal trance.

Choosing the transpersonal countdown instead of the traditional countdown, Lena then laid back and got comfortable. Conducting the countdown (utilizing Lena's own intentions and vocabulary), I spoke the words that would direct Lena to her safe place. Acknowledging her arrival, Lena described the beautiful Pennsylvania woods of her childhood. Her safe place was a cornfield near the backyard of her home. Lingering in the field, she experienced the blazing colors of a fall sunset: the east coast crisp, autumn air.

Asked if she would like to now experience her sacred place, Lena agreed, finding herself in a beautiful bamboo forest. Traveling a bit further, she found herself in a beautiful garden with a waterfall. I asked Lena if she was ready to invite in her spirit-guide. What transpired next was a phenomenon I could never have imagined.

Slowly, Lena began to speak:

"Yes, I see her. Today, she looks older than I've always believed her to be. She has aged beautifully. She is kneeling down beside me. She is so wise. I hear her now speak to me."

"You've known me. I am no stranger."

"I am straining, confused. I'm trying to remember other times, places where I might have known Kuan Yin. In this trance, however, I'm only focused on the now," explained Lena.

"Look beyond what this world offers." Kuan Yin instructed.

"Laid out before Kuan Yin is a beautiful oriental carpet with intricate design," described Lena:

"Watching her suddenly lift the carpet, I hear Kuan Yin say, 'Seek out another place beyond this earth. Be in the now. Where you are right now is what is important. Slow down. Everything is too chaotic. Lay down everything you need to do.'

"She is holding a beautiful vial. I know it holds a liquid that reminds people of their oneness, and makes them feel lighter and aligned with spirit. It is a stress-relieving ointment."

Kuan Yin then concluded for the day:

"You love confections. They remind you of the sweetness of life. Take caution, however, not to overindulge. Too much of any substance can create an imbalance. You're not just your bodies, you know. Keep your spirit connection. Gravity and chemicals are more influential upon the body when one is not connected with spirit. Connection with spirit can even help with certain genetic and hormonal limits."

In the weeks and months to come, I believed this was no accident; that somehow Lena was able to bring from her hypnotic trance to waking reality, highly relevant information; wisdom to assist our lives. Witness and scribe to this sage discussion between Lena and her muse, Kuan Yin, I believed that something spiritually monumental was unfolding before my very eyes.

2
My Intention to Meet Kuan Yin Created Her

April 1, 2004: "There is no Wrong Choice."
-*Kuan Yin*

While EEG frequencies explain much of the phenomenon encountered during trance and dreams, a strictly scientific approach to human consciousness is probably not sufficient to explain what happened to my client, Lena, during the year of 2004.

Throughout history there have been crossroads, times and cultures where emergent *Guides*: visionaries and healers, those who through natural gifts, prayer or trance possess a direct link, channel with spirit. Indeed, is it the channel or the spirit who chooses? And what might be the reasons for such a choice?

Sometimes it is karmic. The channel may have known the spirit personality in another life. They may also have some unfinished business together, a karmic need to once again meet.

Another possible reason for such a choice is the channel's sincere desire to know truth. Such *focused intent* influences, attracts a muse or entity from *the other side* to come forth.

So strong was Lena's intent to meet with Kuan Yin, that from her earliest hypnosis session, she could effortlessly contact and converse with the Deity. While Lena often doubted that Kuan Yin would ever again visit with her, the Deity never once failed to come:

"Kuan Yin is energy manifested into form. She comes to me because of my intention and hers. My intention to meet her *created* her."

During a later exchange, Lena asks Kuan Yin, "Why am I able to have such a good connection with you? Do we have some special karmic connection together?"

"Oh yes. On the earth plane, long ago," replies Kuan Yin "You worshipped my image many times. For your energy, your karmic path, I'm your greatest connection."

"She, Kuan Yin, became very attached to me. She looked out for me. Some are assigned to a Deity. I have been assigned Kuan Yin and it means that my energy force is congruent with the way Kuan Yin is expressed in the world."

In the following visitation, Lena discovers herself once again back in the bamboo forest, sensing Kuan Yin's loving presence. In their second meeting together, it is becoming apparent that a rhythm: an effortless and natural flow is steadily developing between Lena and Kuan Yin.

***

Lena had previously scheduled our time together to be a half-hour earlier. However, between then and now, several unexpected engagements and responsibilities had come up, making meeting at this later hour necessary.

Now, lying back and letting go of the day's concerns, Lena prepares to go into a trance. Having delineated her goals for today, Lena's concern is how to better understand decision-making, how to prioritize her life. Desiring, as well, guidance about certain health issues and simplicity as a way of life, Lena informs me she is ready to be counted down to her sacred place:

"I'm in the bamboo forest, again," begins Lena, explaining her hypnotic arrival at her sacred place. "I see the waterfall. Near the waterfall is a beautiful white silk cushion with Chinese flowers embroidered upon it. Kuan Yin has invited me to sit upon the cushion. She sits down next to me and lays out on a table what appear to be three tarot cards. Painted upon the first one is beautiful shiny black porcelain vase with cherry blossoms. I'm enjoying the marvelous detail of the pink cherry blossoms," comments Lena, deep in trance.

"Suddenly, I'm seeing the trees that grow outside the building where I work. Somehow, I know that this particular tarot card represents my work environment. Illustrated on the next tarot card is a very green plant, maybe a Philodendron. Somehow, I know this card represents my home environment.

The third card is the most disconcerting. It shows a blackened, bare branch, maybe representing the American contractors, the torture victims in Iraq. It is a symbol for the tragedies and suffering occurring in war. However, it is also a symbol for my bad shoulder and my physical pain.

Kuan Yin is laughing now. She wants me to choose from the three cards. I'm asking Kuan Yin, 'What's the right thing to do?'"

"There is no wrong choice," insists Kuan Yin. "You believe there is not enough time, not enough of you to go around. You will understand your own value when you realize you're as worthy when doing one thing as when trying to do many things. It's a *Western* disease. Sad," laments Kuan Yin.

"Kuan Yin's face is changing before me. I don't quite comprehend what is happening. I am suddenly feeling physically *slammed*, shocked," Lena exclaims.

"I'm aware that somewhere in the world, something awful is happening. I see the dead contractors. These are the same men who were recently written about in the international newspapers. They had been hung on the bridge and then tortured by Iraq insurgents."

"It is not a matter of how much pain or suffering one experiences that deems one as worthy," Kuan Yin emphasizes. "It is not how productive one is, either. These are unfortunate beliefs. Simplicity is your life lesson."

Commentary: One's Point of Intention Is One's Attraction Point

Compassion at the level personified by Kuan Yin is not some luxury sentiment that might be expressed towards others at the appropriate moment. Indeed, it is at the very core of our survival. And as Kuan Yin's Law of Compassion is intimately connected with all daily choices and emotions, such compassionate feelings on the part of the ego will join and expand the great rhapsody of light and sound stretching beyond any time/space constraints.

"Do unto others as you would have them do unto you." This ancient Law of Compassion maxim emphasizing compassion and generosity demonstrates that when compassion is at the forefront of consciousness, one will receive back a multitude of blessings, finally culminating in a release from fear.

During any given day, you experience various thoughts and emotions and their resulting intentions. These numerous radiating energy points represent one's *Points of Intention*. Combined with affirmations, they create powerful magnetically charged patterns that expand or contract.

The earth and all its wonders constantly offer an opportunity to identify with joyful spontaneity and abundance. You have the choice, right now, to align your emotions with the biological optimism that surrounds you. Gazing out upon a verdant and peaceful landscape allows your very Core to receive the green restorative energy of the earth: the infinite compassion constantly surrounding you.

Kuan Yin is the crown jewel representing that part of ego capable of having endless love and compassion. It is that personal dimension able to feel Oneness with another ego and nature. Of course, ego inhabits that unique biological position enabling it to choose endless compassion or revenge.

3
Lifetimes to Tell

April 8, 2004: "Look at your palms. They are a record of your life story. There are many reasons you came to earth. Lifetimes to tell! The reasons are intricate, intertwined. The ridges running across your palms are there because you've helped so many."
-*Kuan Yin*

Agreeing, for now, to try and meet on a weekly basis, Lena told me she was pleased the way the first and second sittings had gone. While she didn't recall much, if any, of the information, she confessed she'd felt extremely refreshed after each of her trances. After tape-recording each meeting, I would send a copy (via email) to Lena. For today's trance, Lena had requested (just as we were ending the previous chapter), "How can I train myself to lovingly stay focused upon just one task?"

Now, having attained her trance state and continuing with this theme, Lena finds herself once again in the sacred bamboo garden. Speaking slowly, she comments:

"Yes. Distractions make it difficult for me to stay focused. I want to help people. However, I'm distracted by all the choices. When I was a child, I had to do chores in order to receive an allowance, before I did my homework. Instead of just telling me they didn't have enough money, my parents allowed me to go on doing the chores. I was expected to continue doing the chores and not complain, even during summer vacation."

"What are you experiencing, just now?" I inquire.

"Some pain in my heart and my stomach. I feel *bruised*. My heart aches and I have profound hurt, exhaustion. It's as if this pain is *beyond* my body, *beyond* any physical or emotional level. It is in my *soul*. Children are resilient. I've heard it said," recollects Lena. "And yet, I wonder if it is actually as true as people might believe. One's childhood experiences chip at one's soul. Hopes, dreams, aspirations! All can eventually become depleted. It seems that nothing is ever enough. Nothing is good enough.

I know I'm a people pleaser. Even as a child, I believed it was my responsibility to hold the family together. But nothing I did was ever enough. I still want to make a difference. Now, as an adult, I want to hold the "human family" together.

Maybe I just absorbed my mother's despair. I remember even as a very young child going out into the cornfield behind my house and shaking my fist at the sky. I would cry, 'Why did you put me here?'"

Suddenly, Lena hears Kuan Yin's comforting voice:

"Look at your palms. They're a record of your life story. There are many reasons you came to earth. Lifetimes to tell! The reasons are intricate, intertwined. The ridges running across your palms are there because you've helped so many.

You're here (on earth) at the right time. There are many positive reasons for your incarnation. You are learning compassion and determination. You fight for compassion for the masses! I am sorry for the children's suffering."

(Here, Kuan Yin may be referring not only to Lena's childhood, but also the suffering of the children of poverty and war).

"Sometimes it is hurt which propels a person in a positive direction. Your humanity is having a profound impact upon your own children. It is so profound that you will come to understand how such a positive impact can overcome suffering.

Try not to focus upon the bad news. Such a focus causes you to concentrate upon your own suffering. Because of your humanity, it will take a strong, consistent effort to overcome focusing upon suffering.

You shook your fist, but this was long before you were able to give your gifts. Rather, look at your life as only a piece, one image in an entire role of film."

"I'm witnessing a long film strip," describes Lena. "Kuan Yin is showing me how our lives are but one segment of the whole film. She says I need to value myself, my efforts. If I don't value myself, then my efforts will never feel like enough. Kuan Yin continues to say that I'm putting too much emphasis on suffering and not enough on my good deeds.

Now, she is showing me a scale and the scale is off-balance. She's reminding me that everyone can access what they need from the *other side*."

"It is vital to living!" ordains Kuan Yin. "Like blood in the body. This earth plane is often stuck upon God looking a certain way and having certain teachings. God comes to us in many forms and with many teachings. Fixated upon the "old teachings", beliefs, the message can get stuck in a certain age, possibly devolving into *re-crucifixion*. Earth's spirituality should be evolving," decrees Kuan Yin.

Commentary: The Symbiotic Relationship between Intention and Attention

Above, Kuan Yin has instructed Lena that she may choose to concentrate her attention away from any "bad news" and in a positive direction. *Points of Intention* can gather into a specific vibration attracting expansive or limiting reality-parameters. The logical follow-up to evaluating one's Points of Intention is noticing where one's attention is focused. Providing specific visualizations and meditations, Kuan Yin demonstrates how *focused intent* can assist and accelerate the attraction of beneficial personal as well as mass (energy community) realities.

Identify the goals and passions that currently inspire you. The key to successfully doing this is to be in what Kuan Yin calls your "moment-to-moment" consciousness: an intensely-focused mind state that can offer solutions for many of life's conundrums. Indeed, you may discover (when entering this state), an untapped universe of words and phrases.

Understand also that the thoughts, words and actions you project upon the world can be attracted back to you. Transmuting blame and anger into blessings for others is one of the most potent and beneficial things you can do for others, and by extension, yourself.

What are some of the most powerful thoughts and words in the universe? Kuan Yin's spiritual teachings on compassion and Oneness could remedy the "better than", "not enough" and "survival of the fittest" beliefs responsible for much of the suffering on earth. Acknowledging that reality is eternity, knowledge and bliss can help us to realize a vibration of peace, equality (acceptance of differences) and prosperity.

4
"I Know the Whole Story"

April 15, 2004: "You must acknowledge and experience this part of the universe. Karma is intricate—too vast. You would with your limited human senses, consider it too unfair. But you have tools to really, truly love. Loving the children is very important. But love everyone as you would love your children."
-*Kuan Yin*

Lena began today's episode in the usual way. Allowing herself to be counted down to her sacred place, she found herself once again conversing with Kuan Yin in the bamboo garden:

"I'm aware that Kuan Yin comes to me in various guises. Sometimes it is with the sweet naiveté of a young girl and sometimes with a wizened smile and wisps of graying hair. Whatever form she takes, she is always the one watching over the mothers and children of this great earth. And always, she clutches her precious vase. Vessel of alchemy!

Sometimes I feel helpless about the war. Do we pray? Light candles? Now, I see a young woman coming forth now from the bamboo clearing. Standing near a waterfall, she is wearing a long flowing robe. Perhaps my eyes deceive me. Maybe it is the sunlight, which makes her appear so radiant.

She looks so young. Sweet smile, raven hair swept back; she lovingly returns my stare. Touching the incredible fabric of her gown, I'm aware of its luxurious softness. It is like touching a thousand feathers. My eyes follow the long trail of her gown as it descends into a black and starry universe. Desperately clasping the gown, as if it were the edge of a cliff, I notice how my body is now cradled, supported by it.

She is energy manifested into form. She seems to come to me because of my intention and hers. My intention to meet her *created* her. A deity! A real force! She is happy, confident. She is high above the earth consciousness. There are others like her," explains Lena, deep in trance.

The center of my body is glowing, now. It's a peachy red like bright red poppies, warm and fiery. She and I are passing over the earth. Looking down on the earth, it's as if I'm in a spaceship. Suddenly, a great hole opens in Kuan Yin's gown. I want to say a prayer, to send a blessing to the earth; a great love energy. Kuan Yin wants me to know, however, that all the people will not experience the love energy in the same way. Some will be comforted. Some will be changed. And some will be confused and even angry."

"I must tell you," Kuan Yin commences, "In this place, the Middle East, where the feminine force is so often pushed away, such a powerful prayer can cause men to yearn for their mothers."

"Knowing this and knowing my former disenchantment with prayer, I still beg Kuan Yin to send this love. Answering my prayer, she spreads the energy far and wide. The earth reciprocates, sending love, energy back in our direction. There is a feeling of oneness, the earth is glad to see me."

"Civilization began in the Middle-East," professes Kuan Yin, hurriedly trying to answer all of Lena's questions.

"Certain areas of the earth have more conflict than others. The Middle East *holds* an energy humans are trying to work out. The reason pain exists is because of some of the choices you, as humans, have made. Humans always have a great freedom to choose."

"Now I see a paint box," comments Lena. "Some of the colors are clear, some are murky. The colors of paint are metaphors for the choices we all have in this world! I see this. I know this. Yet, I still have more questions to ask Kuan Yin. Innocent people, little children are involved in this war. Why?"

Kuan Yin then replies with great patience and wisdom: "Your senses (as a human being) are relatively limited. Smells, tastes—there are dimensions you are not capable of knowing in the earth dimension.

You are very upset about the suffering of others. Yet, it is your concern (your instinct to protect others) that is creating a blockage to understanding the enormous complexity. You think that I'm insensitive. Work on your relationship with suffering. *Hold* the energy in a non-judgmental way. I'm happy you can meet with me. People have to ask, to *care* in order to see me! They must have an intention to seek.

While I represent nurturing, compassion, I'm not like some of the other saints. Different saints and demigods assist different energies. They come to people in their differing forms and at varying stages of human evolution. There are any numbers of gods and demigods, endless compassion for those who wish to attain a state of consciousness: comfort beyond their current level.

There are the *lower* saints as well. They are the beginning stage and may be closer to the human realm as they feel sorry for people. But humans don't need pity. They need *empathy*, detached compassion. And you, my dear one, don't have to endure the slings and arrows of this world."

"Consciousness does evolve. Kuan Yin is assuring me of that," relays Lena.

"Now, I see newer energies, smaller orbs of consciousness. Kuan Yin is telling me they are like cells starting out. It is not good to be *too* psychically open in a sometimes- difficult world. If someone is too open, they are vulnerable to mental or physical illness and can possibly destroy themselves. Sometimes you need to comprehend with your senses: to develop the words to understand."

Admitting she can no longer restrain herself, Lena informs me that she must ask Kuan Yin the following question:

"But there are so many people being killed. Why?"

"They've only experienced one part of their entire existence: the suffering. It is not the end of their existence. They will continue on. The only reason for suffering is not being connected, believing one is estranged from the universe. This is a very young planet, the life forms are young," assures Kuan Yin.

"But why are we stuck here?"

"You must acknowledge and experience this part of the universe. Karma is intricate, too vast. You would (with your limited human senses) consider it too unfair. But you have tools to really, truly love. Loving the children is very important. But love *everyone* as you would love your children."

(Periodically elaborating on its relevance throughout the text, Kuan Yin's definition of karma departs from traditional cause and effect theory: the total moral sum of an individual's life, determining the circumstances of one's next life. Stating that: "we've already lived all our lives", Kuan Yin stresses that it

is the accumulated expansive and/or limiting beliefs (from the simultaneous, past, present and future) creating "made-up stories" about oneself and, thus, reality.)

"Now, she is showing me her bottle of healing medicine," comments Lena. "Kuan Yin and I are journeying back through the universe. I'm coming back through the hole at the end her gown. It is like the Milky Way. She tells me I'll feel the effect of the healing water in a few days."

"You work so hard. How amazing of you. You have trials but you can always come to me. You can offer a lot back to the earth because you've lived on the earth. I am showing you the planet that you will be assigned to. There are a lot of entities like you. They've come, like you, to learn so they can teach others how to care for and help the earth. To do this, one must live on the earth, be in an earth body."

Lena remains silent for a moment; apparently deeply engaged in viewing the planet Kuan Yin has described. Informing me of my next incarnation (or assignment), Kuan Yin continues:

"Hope is assigned to a different planet."

"I can barely see the planet you are assigned to, Hope;" concedes Lena. "It is very light and ethereal and very far away."

Upon returning to waking consciousness, Lena explained that while channeling the above passages, it was as if she was looking down upon a giant map of Iraq. Amazed that the map had suddenly transformed, she realized she was subsequently peering down at the actual geographical location of the Fertile Crescent. (Existing over 6000 years ago; inhabiting this specific geographical location, the Sumerian's are believed by many, to be the progenitors of civilization.)

Commentary: You Have Great Freedom to Choose

Many of Kuan Yin's preceding Ascended Master's have so indicated that humans have the ability to exercise control over reality much more then was perhaps formerly understood. Kuan Yin's explanation of free will in a quantum universe helps clarify certain other teachings on Kuan Yin's Law of Compassion. One's beliefs and the vibrations they create potentially (depending upon their consistency), magnetize reality-parameters from all comparable Evolutionary Potentials.

Free will to choose one's thoughts and actions; to transcend any limiting soul (reincarnation) agreements forms the basis of Kuan Yin's spiritual bulwark. Desiring us to understand and master the powerful forces within us that can innately direct, attract and transform energy, Kuan Yin's spiritual doctrine is as authentic as it is compelling.

Kuan Yin espouses: *"all experiences must exist"*. She also states: *"you've already lived all of your lives"*. In terms of Kuan Yin's Law of Compassion, the above statements imply that the preponderance of events and objects one is currently experiencing have accumulated from the probable past and future. What is our redemption? Through skillfully wielding our innate free will, those events and objects that we choose to energetically align with can eventually be expressed as the *Personal Present*.

I want to emphasize that seemingly straightforward Kuan Yin precepts must be patiently practiced and then incorporated into one's daily routine, to effectively and permanently *rewire* any congested 'pathways'. Through incorporating focused intent, self-responsibility and a willingness to turn obstacles into opportunities, anything is possible. Similar to Kuan Yin transporting Lena through a black hole and out into a universe of swirling stars and galaxies, you are suddenly on the *other side*, having 'crossed-home' to your birthright.

5
Shrouded Kuan Yin

April 22, 2004: "See the power of the mothers' love? It is their right to wail."
-*Kuan Yin*

Attentive to my voice counting her down to a profound trance state, anxious to once again meet with Kuan Yin, Lena finds herself in her accustomed sacred place near the bamboo grove and waterfall. Soon after her arrival, Lena realizes Kuan Yin has come to her today in a new guise, as beautiful and serene ebony Kuan Yin:

"Staring into her deep, steady eyes, I notice that Kuan Yin's shoulders are draped with a large patchwork quilt. Each quilted patch bares a face of the fallen: American and Iraqi soldiers stitched carefully and lovingly into this cloth of death," elucidates Lena.

"Quickly come," Kuan Yin beckons.

"I am aware that Kuan Yin is eager to begin the journey. This time, however, I do not want to follow."

"We haven't time for chatter," Kuan Yin beckons, somewhat impatiently.

"I'm noticing that on the sleeve of her patchwork gown, she wear's the face of just one soldier," describes Lena.

"Kuan Yin is pointing and I look down, down into a small pond. In the pond I see a reflection, a soldier's face and hat. I feel his fear as I *move through* his forehead into the hot, dry Iraq desert. I'm standing on the ground. I don't want to go any further. 'Why must I be here?'" Lena passionately asks Kuan Yin.

Still cloaked in the patchwork quilt, Kuan Yin replies, "It is not important. Look, look. Give me a chance to explain."

"I trust her and go. I see a man in a field. There are primitive huts, sheep and chickens. Maybe the huts hold the animals or the people. I'm not sure. They are made of straw and mud with corrugated metal roofs. Now I see a man riding on a horse. Drowning out the sweetness of everyday life, an American chopper drones loudly overhead:

'I don't want to be a part of your quilt of dead soldiers'", Lena suddenly protests: interrupting her normal trance pace.

Now Lena exclaims, "I hear the mother's wail. These are mothers of American soldiers. Yanking, ripping at the woman's cloak, they can't tear off the pictures. Kuan Yin watches calmly. I'm beginning to comprehend how she is neither aloof nor is she uncaring of the events taking place."

Continuing, Lena then asks, "what is the point of showing me this?'"

Following a prolonged and emotionally charged silence, Kuan Yin methodically responds to Lena's question.

"Karma. People can consciously choose and direct it. Most of the soldiers believed they had no other choice so they went this route."

"What do you want me to know besides this? Why did I have to come down here?"

Lena pauses for a moment and then continues, resigned to describing what she is now experiencing:

"I'm seeing Kuan Yin shape-shift for a moment. However, for the most part she remains in her steady, powerful form as a cloaked, dark-skinned Kuan Yin. She tells me this is just one of the many forms she can take, one of her many manifestations. Kuan Yin continues to sit tranquilly upon her throne. Meanwhile, the mothers beg her and tug passionately at her robe of death. Yet, she remains the most powerful mother of all."

"So much anguish. Look at the power of love," denotes Kuan Yin.

"Suddenly I understand the power of the mothers' love," whispers Lena. "I know that it is the most powerful love in the world."

"But why drag *me* here?' Lena again questions. "Do you want to invoke some kind of feeling? How can I use this experience to change the world? I'm just one person."

After another prolonged interlude, Kuan Yin patiently answers Lena's question:

"This war is going to change because of the mothers' love. I can't save everyone. And I can only utilize humanity's own resources, which is love and free will. I can't use any force that does not come from within humans to change the war. Earth is in a certain karmic cycle. Most of the leaders carrying out this karmic cycle we're presently experiencing are men."

"So why try? Why try to save the world if we are in a karmic cycle?" Beseeches Lena; trying to comprehend Kuan Yin's words.

Lena now informs me she can still hear the mother's wail. She is also still witnessing the mothers of the fallen soldiers clutching at Kuan Yin's long, patchwork cloak.

"Is there any small thing I can do about the war?"

(Apprising me of the constantly shifting dynamics of her trance, Lena explains that she is experiencing herself back in her original trance location of the Iraqi desert. Suddenly, she sees a group of American fighter tanks coming into view.)

"No one is here. Maybe I see some shepherds in the field, now. It is near sunset and the sun is going down. I see crude, connected huts. The windows are framed with wood. Near the huts is a large rectangular hole in the ground. Refusing to look, I sense someone might be buried there.

'Why show me this? Isn't death pointless?'" Lena entreats Kuan Yin.

"It's not pointless, it wasn't pointless," interrupts another new, and as yet unidentified, speaker.

Lena now explains that the new persona is that of the dead soldier: the one she'd suspected was buried in the shallow rectangular grave.

"But, you were so scared," Lena remarks to the soldier.

"That's not what I'll remember," replies the soldier.

Incredulous, Lena demands, "Why, wasn't it pointless?"

"I served my purpose on the earth. My death is going to make an impact on my son, on people. I'm at peace with my death," assures the soldier.

"The men are shouting, now. They have found someone wrapped like a mummy down in the hole," proclaims Lena. "What does this all symbolize? War can be so cruel, brutal."

"Again I say! The spirits will try to find and connect with family members. He (the soldier) connected with *you* in your dreams. This is one of your gifts, to help those passing over to connect with loved ones, to complete the process."

"I see the soldier again," explains Lena. "He is at peace, because he knows his son will do something great. He knows his son is great hearted: loving and forgiving. Knowing his progeny will grow to be someone important, even historical; he's very proud, even as he watches his young son from his grave."

Suddenly addressing me, Lena comments:

"I remember when I was getting my massage earlier today. I saw hints, a glimpse of what this next meeting was going to be like, that Kuan Yin would be dressed in a patchwork quilt robe."

"I'm not aloof or callous," insists Kuan Yin. I know the *whole story*."

"I'm seeing the mother's clutching her robe, once again," Lena elucidates.

"Do you see their anguish?" inquires Kuan Yin.

"The women consumed by grief?"

"Yes. Isn't it potent?"

"Yes, it is quite potent," agrees Lena. "Kuan Yin is pouring the elixir from her vial, now."

"You see," decrees Kuan Yin. "Anguish is transformed into pure love. It's alchemy! I won't allow the anguish to continue. The potion turns it into pure love."

"I wish I could remember these words when I'm in my own anguish," laments Lena.

"You can. Just always value my words. The best motivation is valuing my words."

"I'm focused once again on the women who are still wailing for their sons," Lena confides.

"It is there right to wail," insists Kuan Yin.

"Could you send them my love?" inquires Lena of Kuan Yin.

"Yes."

Commentary: Love, Free Will and Kuan Yin's Law of Compassion

Kuan Yin's primary message is that the love and abundance of the universe is available 24/7. Misguided beliefs and projections can, however, pose significant setbacks to even a sage mindset. Most individuals will experience (at some time) a fearful mindset. A prevalent limiting "made up story" is that one is unworthy of receiving all the good things in life. However, one always has the option to believe that one is worthy. If you are having difficulty accepting this, you should probably find out why.

Fulfilling or unfulfilling emotional patterns can originate and then solidify from beliefs having been formed and developed over lifetimes. Denial and repressed emotions can act like a logjam, preventing the creative force from expressing itself in a positive way. Repressive patterns likely spiral into the flip side of denial: blame.

Genuine resolution for these entrapping cycles can only come through completely loving oneself and believing in one's worthiness. When purely experienced, the potent force of Kuan Yin's *Love and Forgiveness Principle* could attract the people and events that will assist you in reaching your highest goals.

Kuan Yin's spiritual toolkit brims with interactive strategies and techniques that can help one undo any limiting cycle. Through prayer, affirmation, assimilation of the Kuan Yin canons, chakra work, visualization, meditation, and striving to have a loving and compassionate nature, one may access the infinite potential of her/his creative and ingenious nature.

Draped in a cloak emblazoned with faces of the fallen soldiers; symbolizing the power of motherly love and compassion, *Shrouded Kuan Yin* assures us that motherly love is the most potent energy of all.

We can't force others to come to our way of believing. However, we can love them just as surely as we can love ourselves in an understanding and compassionate way. Only through incorporating this form of love; the unconditional love a mother has for her child, may the Gordian knot (that some have bound their souls in), be untangled.

6
"All of Life Is a Prayer"

May 6, 2004: "You see? I still am my original form. It didn't *destroy* me."
-*Kuan Yin*

Family obligations had forced both of us to skip our scheduled meeting for the previous Thursday. When we finally got together again, disturbing allegations of prisoner abuse occurring at the US-run prison, "Abu Ghraib" had recently surfaced in the news. Additionally, Iraqi Insurgents had purportedly stepped up their bombing campaigns of strategic areas in Iraq.

Admitting her existential despair—her mounting frustration concerning world events, Lena was enthusiastic to once again visit with Kuan Yin:

"I've been helped by Kuan Yin, and yet I always look forward to learning more."

Easily and effortlessly Lena was counted down to her trance state. There, she discovered a new and beautiful "sacred place":

"I don't know why, but I'm in a redwood forest, today. It is very beautiful and once again Kuan Yin has come to me. She is in, yet, another form. I see her today as a white porcelain statue. Statuesque, rigid she is nevertheless able to advance forward towards where I am standing. Quickly approaching, now, Kuan Yin now is near the redwood tree and me.

I see the long train of her gown flowing down, down until it flows into a hole at the base of the redwood trunk. I'm aware it is another entrance, yet another doorway to consciousness. Now the train of her gown is flowing out of the hole and into the universe. Her long robe has made a heart around the planet Jupiter. It is very much like the Milky Way.

I'm at the base of one of the trees and I feel like Alice in Wonderland. My hands are holding effortlessly onto the end of her robe. Her robe reminds me of something, like the silver umbilical cord spiritualists always talk about.

Remember, Hope, how they say the silver umbilical cord represents our connection to our divinity?"

"*I do,*" I reply, recalling certain books on the subject.

"Still clutching the silver cord, I see how Kuan Yin's face is very near. She is staring lovingly at me. 'Why am I here?'" I ask Kuan Yin.

"Kuan Yin is showing me a beautiful nebula in the universe. Suddenly I'm swirling around like a million stars in a galaxy."

"I made the nebulas small enough so you'll feel like a bee inside a flower," explains Kuan Yin.

"I am experiencing spectacular formations and re-formations, the birth and death of stars. Space is so peaceful and quiet. Kuan Yin is sitting on the long trail of cloth extending from her gown. Pulling me close to her, she is comforting me like a mother would her child. Today she is very young and motherly, holding me as if I were an infant, looking at me, really *seeing* me. I'm aware that she loves me just the way I am. I am not used to this kind of attention. I can feel her strong intent as she gazes upon me.

Kuan Yin wants to (if an individual is willing to receive) give people loving and healing energy. She's putting that energy in *me*. She says it is *love.*"

"We send them love and see what happens," Kuan Yin explains.

"Suddenly, I'm witnessing an orb of love energy going out over a map of Iraq. Kuan Yin is calling for this prayer with great intention," relays Lena.

"There will be different reactions, you see," continues Kuan Yin. "We had to send the love and it is good. Love is showing the goodness of so many of the Iraqi people; even though they're considered the enemy and even though they've been abused and humiliated. A new compassion has come their way. That is what prayer is. Many don't understand prayer. It is important to understand what prayer is. It is sent out as strong intention and energy. I want you, Lena; to get unstuck, send focused intent. Be detached with the results. Trust!"

"That's incredible," comments Lena. "I suppose if prayer requires focused intent then *all of life is a prayer.* Kuan Yin wants to sit with me, for a moment, in silence."

"*OK. I'll just check in with you from time to time,*" I reassure Lena.

"I don't really know what I'm seeing. I just see all kinds of shapes and forms of Kuan Yin," continues Lena. "Now I'm witnessing a scene of Hiroshima, a great mushroom cloud. She's inside it. Now it is inside of *her*. Suddenly, it explodes in her body and she absorbs, *becomes* the energy. That's her message for this chapter. Nothing can harm her. Even the most devastating force is changed, *softened* so that people will grow even when experiencing complete destruction. She's not afraid to merge with the most fearsome creations."

"You see," announces Kuan Yin, "I am still in my original form. It didn't *destroy* me."

Transcribing Kuan Yin and Lena's amazing discourse, I try, in vain, to visualize the phenomenon Lena has just described. Returning to pen and paper, I realize Lena has been silent for a while. Receiving another communication, she then resumes speaking:

"I'm reminded of how passionate Kuan Yin is about the importance of being human on this earth," continues Lena.

"It's the most important thing in your existence," ordinates Kuan Yin. "Your existence is eternal. This phase (of your soul) is so important because you learn so much in human form. This is where the individual's 'spark' or existence can expand into bigger, more powerful *energies*, not *entities*.

Entities are *closed* systems whereas *energies* are *open* systems," differentiates Kuan Yin.

"Some energies are not as potent. The only way to develop a potent energy is to spend an existence on the earth. There, one can develop a compassionate nature so that when passing onto other dimensions, one can be of help. When one leaves one's earth body one will need to fully understand compassion to be helpful, effective.

On earth, you are encapsulated in flesh. During the first episode I wanted to take you on a little tour of the universe. No soul is forced into an assignment upon the earth. Instead they go to their 'rightful space'. When you leave the earth you have a lot more power. It won't be *ego-based* power. Rather it will be beyond ego, beyond good and evil. In fact, 'evil' is just a label as everything is intermixed. The pendulum just appears to swing back and forth."

"Kuan Yin is chastising me," Lena reveals. "She wants me to really value my life here on earth. She knows I haven't completely accepted it. I don't fully feel it, yet. I've resisted the human condition. She wants me to feel the full spectrum of humanity and not be afraid. Kuan Yin says it's the one thing we need to be truly effective in helping the earth when we're not human anymore. She wants me to throw myself into being human.

Suddenly, I see Kuan Yin as a bird with a Kuan Yin head. She is just walking along on my arm. She's dwarfing herself in order to make me feel big. She's resting on my injured arm, now. Is there something healing about a white bird? Kuan Yin looks interesting as a bird. Maybe she is a dove of peace. She reminds me the only way I'll not be afraid to be fully human is to visit with her from time to time."

"Many who perpetrate war are not yet in their full humanity. They hate their own humanness as much as they appear to hate others. Certain religions can be harmful for the same reason. Humanity, then, is misunderstood. It's a powerful place to be when it is fully experienced. However, it is often underestimated," explains Kuan Yin. "Unless one fully experiences his or her humanity, one will have to experience earth again and again. One will have to repeat the lessons offered here upon the earth. It is possible that one need not have to reincarnate. Many don't live up to their full potential because they're afraid of death. I want to emphasize here that <u>only</u> the body dies. People get too attached (to their physicality). But, they have to. One's consciousness must be fairly strong in order for the soul's desire to continue. The more we feel our humanity, the more help we can give and the more joy we can create."

Lena now informs me that Kuan Yin is telling her how she appreciates Lena's humanitarian efforts and that when Lena is no longer in a physical body, she will be doing more of the same.

"I'm having a little difficulty understanding Kuan Yin," continues Lena. "It's a different language she speaks and I need to always be careful I'm interpreting what she says correctly.

She's showing me a person running with sandbags. She's telling me that when the person finally lets-go of the sandbags, he or she is faster, stronger. Oh. I get it! That's what the earth existence is like. In many ways living on earth is an 'artificial' burden. Once one is free of one's body, he or she is not only lighter; one is also stronger, more powerful. I'm reminded of a time when I was a child. I felt so limited. I remember thinking, 'Why can't I just be wherever I want to be and physically not have to walk or use transportation? Why do I have to physically cross the street?'"

"That's why cars and planes were invented," Kuan Yin asserts. "They're physical simulations for 'thinking yourself there'. The humbling experience of the earth experience develops compassion and humility. It's the best thing for you."

Lena continues, saying, "Kuan Yin is really trying to get through to me, to explain a specific concept. In order to illustrate her point, she's moving through many thick energy fields. I guess I never thought the earth plane as very important. She's telling me the greatest misunderstanding is to regard this life as a curse or punishment.

She's shape shifting again, performing amazing fluctuations to show how life isn't stagnant. Our experiences are ever changing, flowing, (so we won't take ourselves too seriously). She's forming something and then something else."

"I neither created it nor am I destroyed by it," proclaims Kuan Yin. "A person can forget that this life is just one picture out of the entire reel of the movie. They could be frightened of the pain because they don't know when it will end. But it wouldn't be so painful if one didn't fear it.

Know this. You can go through disaster and I'll still be here. I'm here for you eternally," reassures Kuan Yin.

"She's transforming into more shapes," remarks Lena: "a stern mother, a playful child. Small and large images! They're just floating there. Kuan Yin wants to tell me so much. Sometimes it feels like she wants to tell me everything at once. She's afraid I won't meet with her again. Her language is a difficult one and I don't always understand what she is trying to tell me. She tells me I can go through disaster and she'll still be here—that she's here for me *eternally*. Hope, she relies on you so much. Wow. Suddenly she's left me and is over by you, Hope. Kuan Yin is right by your side."

Opening her eyes, looking directly at me for the first time in over an hour and a half, Lena says:

"Hope, Kuan Yin is now embracing you."

Commentary: Believing in One's Power and Kuan Yin's Law of Compassion.

Kuan Yin has declared that there is no time: that we've already lived *all* of our lives. As we are so accustomed to thinking in terms of a past, present and future, many would conjecture that such revelations have little relevance to our *realistic* lives.

This is because ego focuses and associates itself almost exclusively with sequential time. One avenue related to its sense of reason and definition of time has caused ego to develop reincarnation theories pivoting upon the precept of sequential time. With its somewhat limited definitions, ego also assumes that in the past, one has accumulated both compassionate and consequential deeds, rewarded or punished through the system traditionally known as *karma*.

Yet, we have visions and dreams. And within the alpha, theta and delta, non-lineal time frameworks, a punishment could just as easily *precede* the consequential act, rendering ego's sequential perception of guilt and punishment incorrect.

Because focusing upon one's limitless potential can elicit feelings of expansiveness whereas fear of death and pain may create feelings of limitation; it could prove helpful for one to continue researching reincarnation and quantum theories.

There is a correlation between Kuan Yin's kaleidoscopic shape shifts and attracting your goals. Within the constructs of particle and multiple universe theories, Kuan Yin's multidimensional forms show the nature of the universe as it actually exists when ego linear selection is removed. The embodiment of dynamic concepts of energy and motion, Kuan Yin represents every probable arrangement of elemental building blocks. Forming immense and infinitesimal self-creations from levels of scale so small as to be undetectable by the human eye, she is the divine expression of matter and energy.

Having their unique and indelible vibrations, thoughts and emotions are intimately associated with molecular processes and the building up and breaking down of matter. Examples of how these are the basis for infinite realities; universes, Kuan Yin's metamorphisms demonstrate evolutions proceeding from the original imprint. Because the mind can hope and because reality is capable of being imagined, focused intent is expressed as infinite multidimensional energetic imprints.

Kuan Yin's transformations show the infinite Evolutionary Potentials available, allowing for endless embellishment of your waking reality. Once you're grounded in your truth through self-evaluation, you can imbue your life with the most apropos and expansive elements.

7
The Breadcrumb Maker

May 14, 2004: "I am making a path of breadcrumbs back to one's true divine and peaceful nature. Every period needs some *breadcrumb-makers*."
-Kuan Yin

Before Lena and I began the countdown today, she remarked on the many profound dreams of the prior week. She'd intuited that they could be previews for today's discussion with Kuan Yin:

"They seemed to be dreams concerned with some important life message. I believe they were ultimately focused upon the dynamics involved in how people are attracted to one another and meet; how human relationships are very magical. All week long, I felt pulled, compelled to find books and images of Kuan Yin. Did you know that historically Kuan Yin has evolved from being a man to a woman?"

"Yes, I've read that how for a very long time Kuan Yin was regarded as male—that only much later was this deity regarded as female."

"I have some more books on the subject that I can show you later," informs Lena.

"OK. I'd be interested in reviewing them."

"I've been feeling Kuan Yin around me the entire week in a kind of in a matter-of-fact way. I've been doing computer searches, finding out as much as I can about her."

"Do you feel Kuan Yin nearby you right now?"

"Yes."

"Will you need a formal hypnosis induction?"

"I think so. Even though I feel her energy near me, hypnosis helps me to achieve greater sense of calm, a receptive state of mind."

Proceeding with our customary countdown, I uttered the words: "Beginning with the number ten, experience going deeper than you ever have before. And isn't it good to know you may experience the trance that is just right for you, today. Nine! The number nine, etc...

And when you reach your sacred place, just begin to describe what you are experiencing."

At that very moment, Lena began to articulate what she was witnessing:

"Kuan Yin is always around water. I see her now. The lotus pond and waterfall are behind her. She is alabaster white, her raven hair swept back with beautiful jeweled combs adorning it. She appears very much like a large statue. She's very still, inanimate.

I go up over the waterfall and I can see the cornfield near the house where I grew up. It is so peaceful. It is where I used to walk to collect my thoughts when I was a young girl. It made a lasting impression on me: the beautiful fields and autumn sunsets. Now, while remembering, enjoying the scent of what some might consider unpleasant odors such as cow manure, I recall that period in my life with great fondness.

I'm not sure why I'm going into these childhood memories. Standing in the field not far from the cows, I feel the wind against my cheek. I'm noticing that everything is focused upon nature and how, indeed, focusing on nature instead of current events can be very positive. Maybe Kuan Yin is showing me an alternative focus to disturbing news events and especially the war.

I'm remembering how it feels to be thirteen or fourteen. It was a wonderful age for me. I felt as though I was coming into my power, transforming from child to adult. It was a time of good feelings. I was suddenly aware that I possessed strengths that I'd never before been aware of; strengths that were separate from my parents.

Kuan Yin wants me to remember those times, because those memories give me strength now. Suddenly I'm having a question rise up in me. How can I be more present for my son? What is the connection between my son and I?

'Help me help him heal,' I say to Kuan Yin. "Every night I hold him and I read him a story. I know these special times together are helping him to heal. Is there more I can do?'

Kuan Yin is pleased with the special quality mothers and sons have together. She says that you know about this, Hope."

Suddenly it is Kuan Yin who is speaking:

"Many don't understand the power of love; that it is there for them if they choose to accept it. Of course, just because it is there, doesn't necessarily mean they'll accept it. Like a seed, it will always be there. Because of free will, humans can accept or reject that love. We, who so much wish to have the love we send; be received, must remain somewhat detached."

Continuing to respond to Lena's questions about parenting, Kuan Yin says almost plaintively:

"You don't always come to me. Stay constant and aware in your love."

Contemplating Kuan Yin's words for a moment, Lena then asks:

"The warrior spirit seems so imbalanced here on earth. How can we heal this? How do I understand it, make peace with it?"

"Unfortunately, there are too few strong leaders, right now. It is like spice. If one adds too much, the dish will taste wrong and maybe even make one ill. Of course, I'm making an analogy to militarism," explains Kuan Yin. "Human emotions and actions can be compared to spice. Spicy dishes can be heavenly to the senses. However, they must be cooked consciously and with skill. Some who participate in war are doing all they know how to do. You can, however, send consciously-directed love and prayers."

"I want to know more about praying, how it works. I'm currently witnessing the soldiers eating their dinner in the mess hall," describes Lena.

"Kuan Yin is covering the soldiers with a transparent veil made of stars, the Milky-Way. She's floating in space above the region of Iraq, covering the whole area with love. But I don't know how to participate. I ask Kuan Yin to send the love for me."

"That's the secret. Your prayer for them is exactly what they need. They're homesick and their hearts ache for motherly love. And remember, militarism can't happen without a dominant mindset, certain perceptions about the world, about other cultures. So many souls, energies have a certain perception of others. They believe they're separate from one another.

Such perceptions can collect into a great energy agreeing upon a specific direction the country will take. The lesson is acceptance of differences. Don't forget you are a part of everything and everything is a part of you."

"I'm suddenly feeling really weak, heavy," confides Lena, in an ever-deepening trance. "Kuan Yin is taking me to a place representing a certain kind of collective consciousness. It is an actual reality but is also symbolic of powerless women living on the earth. I seem to be in Afghanistan (or somewhere resembling Afghanistan) but am also aware this area represents the repressive reality in many parts of the world.

I'm experiencing the intense feelings of defeat in the women. However, I'm also feeling the extreme fear of women by the men. Why are the men so terrified of women? Somehow, they feel vulnerable. Kuan Yin is showing me some kind of divide. One side holds the terrified men. The other side holds the defeated, powerless women. This, for now, is as much as I'm able to interpret."

"There are correct theories by those who've studied spiritual evolution," informs Kuan Yin. I'll bring it to your attention, later through revealing the titles of specific books on this subject. For now, just know that this is very important. If enough people know about this, if every human being could recognize the power of the *Love and Forgiveness Principle* all consciousness on earth would change instantly. Indeed, thoughts can change the course of history. Sometimes, all it takes is enough people knowing about a certain concept.

Rapid changes are coming," portends Kuan Yin. "It's an urgent time for energies to evolve. I don't think of it as a happy time. However, it is an opportunity for some to propel themselves into a kind of purification. The process is being sped up, an acceleration creating awe-inspiring changes affecting every aspect of life. There are a group of souls who are using this time to help propel them forward. This process can be compared to a ship catching the wind in a certain way. Those catching this wind will need to be skillful, knowledgeable and willing to let go, like a navigator or a sailor.

And like a sailor's knowledge and deep respect for the sea, these people will need to know when to *turn the ship* and when to *let go*. Skillful in utilizing the 'winds of these times', they will have me as their sail.

I am making a path of breadcrumbs back to one's true *divine and peaceful* nature. Every historic period needs some *breadcrumb-makers*. It is difficult for some to hear the voices of the Divine Spirit. This may be because some are so invested in material things. I understand. I feel a deep compassion for these human beings. Material things are a temporary relief from pain.

It is time now for you to return to your world, Lena."

"I'm feeling this unbelievable love surrounding Kuan Yin and me. She has such deep, abiding love for humans. All morning I was feeling heaviness; that today's conversation with Kuan Yin would explain and maybe alleviate this feeling."

"Do you need to be counted back up?" I ask.

"Yes, I'm still in such a deep trance. I think that being counted back up will probably be necessary."

Commentary: Catching the *Wind*

Today, physics suggests the plausibility of multiple universes. Such a theory may eventually support the concept of a universe void of time wherein we each experience multiple lifetimes.

How does one reconcile such a precept with traditional definitions of reincarnation; that one is reborn into a succession of lifetimes? According to Kuan Yin, events in all fields of consciousness (including trance and dreams) are valid: that the soul is the eternal voyager in a timeless universe. It is the conscious and unconscious mind's prismatic perceptual abilities that allow us to traverse and shape our in and out of time realities.

While modern physics may provide insights pointing to the multidimensional nature of reality, it is this moment; this life we are presently experiencing that is the most important.

The waking self's main job is to discover how to effectively play the *game* offered here on earth: how to magnetize the most beneficial experiences. Throughout, Kuan Yin insists that when incarnating one's soul is already aware of the possibility that one might become overwhelmed by the sometimes heavy and detrimental consciousness of other humans.

Certainly then, the ego's insulating mindset is necessary and integral to the "grand plan". Development of individuality is a central component for conscious navigation and attraction of reality. That is why Kuan Yin implores us not to "curse the ego".

Inundated by external stimuli and perceived threats, the ego could get lost in "mind chatter" and "made-up stories". It's permissible to sometimes allow the mind to wander. In fact, a daydream now and then can be inspiring. Neglecting to learn the basic premises; how to properly form and direct one's thoughts, though, may cause one to become immersed in repeated limiting and polarized realities.

8
"The Universe Will Bring People Anything They Want"

"Let the magic happen! It is always there. Abundance and love are always there. Believe in the highest good, there is a higher essence to everything."
-*Kuan Yin*

Revered to be among the all-knowing ones; *The Elders*, Kuan Yin has come at this critical historical juncture to share her eternal wisdom. Goddess of Compassion! The one who sees and hears all!

Stating: *"Everyone creates realities based on their own personal beliefs. These beliefs are so powerful that they can create {expansive or entrapping} realities over and over,"* Kuan Yin spiritual insights expound upon the intricacies of Her Law of Compassion and how you can be aligned with your own spiritual depth.

In a world where we are continually barraged by disjointed information, we must determine for ourselves what is personally relevant. Until recently, there have primarily been institutional interpretations, often having the goal of controlling large populations. Kuan Yin's Law of Compassion, compared to many other philosophical movements is a radical departure. Giving form and direction to our lives, it can bring to the fore pre-existing extraordinary potentials that we may have largely ignored. Kuan Yin's starting assumptions for reality are that we attract those people and events from a personal gestalt of beliefs, emotions and intentions.

The absolute Kuan Yin Law of Compassion tenet is that one's beliefs and intentions cause gravitation of similar vibrational thought structures back to the original thought focal point. Throughout, Kuan Yin reminds us that there is no beginning or end: only the universal laws that have been with us forever.

As it is a prerequisite for raising one's vibration, Kuan Yin' *Love and Forgiveness Principle* reigns supreme. The Goddess's compassionate approach does not involve pity. Rather, through practicing her form of empathy: "compassion for the untruth", one can discover how to see beyond any limitations. It also means allowing for the universe to come into one's life and assist. *"The universe will bring people anything they want,"* states Kuan Yin.

Maintaining that we've *"already lived all our lives"*, Kuan Yin stresses that it is accumulated beneficial or unbeneficial beliefs (from the simultaneous, past, present and future) creating "made-up stories" about reality and, thus, ourselves. And while you may recall, (through visions and dreams) other realities, the life you are presently living is, in fact, your "way out" of any self-destructive patterns. Attracting vital universal energies into physical reality, we begin to understand our central role in the "spiritualization of matter".

A minor dream here! A defining life moment there! In our every day life, experiences and dreams are not tied together in a neat bow. The sequence of events is not spelled out for us. Infinite font of wisdom, Kuan Yin, seeks to unsnarl the cosmic web of beliefs entangling humanity. Weaving her intricate tapestry of spiritual insights, Kuan Yin explains how we have the power to reassemble the disparate jigsaw that is a "realistic life". Her specific interactive strategies can render an ordinary drama, spiritual. Integral to the puzzle of life, each piece fits perfectly, culminating as her opus to humanity.

Kuan Yin's Law of Compassion teachings require an understanding and implementation of Her *Law of the Liberation (Spiritualization) of Matter*. As this universal law addresses energy transformation, it is central for comprehending the mechanics involved in attracting or repelling a particular object or event. This Kuan Yin law states: *"The quality and intensity of resonance emanated from a given point is thus attracted back. When one brings spirit into the human realm, it can spiritualize matter. Matter can then become lighter, (indeed liberated), not as dense as before."*

The above definition is but a precursor to the greater Law of Compassion: Self as the focal point for any magnetized realities. We, as all-knowing, vibrational beings, constantly interact with our physical and non-physical surroundings. Indeed, reality-parameters will be magnetized to you through karmic *windows of opportunity* formed by your specific beliefs and intentions. The true definition of karma, therefore, is that it is only your personal beliefs and "made up stories" allowing these into your aura.

If you believe that your life circumstances are a result of traditional cause and effect doctrine, it is crucial that you understand that this belief alone has the potential to create endless cycles of limitation. Kuan Yin advises that instead of worrying about cause and effect, focus upon whatever is *"the most compassionate thing you can do right now and that you are already liberated"*.

During an average day, one may have several opportunities to show compassion. Though compassion and loving kindness are, according to Kuan Yin, humanity's highest emotional expressions, She nevertheless wishes for us to refrain from being "too open" or to assume any limiting "made-up stories". This can be achieved by practicing what the Goddess terms "detached compassion" while also, hopefully, exemplifying the limitless potential existing within us all.

Just as we have the ability to focus our attention towards something, we can also focus *away* from any limiting experiences. Kuan Yin instructs that we are in no way obligated to direct our attention towards "negative news".

If you are experiencing a reality not to your complete satisfaction, examine any limiting beliefs that may have vibrationally-attracted them. Embellish your phrases and visions with those qualities you wish to attract: not the one's you don't.

As it is you who represents the point from which any desire is being emanated, a successful outcome (when applying the *Law of Liberation of Matter*) will depend upon the force of your *focused intent*. An example might be prayer or stating a beneficent wish for someone. One's strong emotional involvement and focus will play a crucial role in determining a successful outcome.

If desires are not stated clearly and in the *Present Positive,* however, this same law can also cause a desired object or event to be forever out of reach. Imagine that you are watching a television program through the TV screen. Or it could be a beautiful view through your plate glass window. Ego tends to insist that in either case, the glass (to a greater degree) separates the program or view from you. Yet, this vision has entered (through the mind's miraculous structures for sight and perception) your consciousness. Is it not now an integral part of you? The same is true of any concept. Naturally, you will want to select those concepts that are most beneficial and relevant to your goals.

As Kuan Yin's teachings must inevitably all work in harmony together, please do not assume that this is necessarily a linear process or that there is some specific end point. Examine your own beliefs and the circumstances of your life. Are you grateful for what you have? Or do you persist with the "not enough" or "survival of the fittest" mindsets? If you are constantly worrying about the future, believing you haven't enough resources, you risk not savoring what Kuan Yin terms your 'moment-to-moment' consciousness.

Kuan Yin has espoused twenty-one spiritual precepts. Combined, they form the metaphysical scaffolding for the theories discussed herein:

1. Personal reality is a result of one's mindset and "made up stories": an intimate and unique gestalt of beliefs and their resulting intentions, emotions and vibrations.

2. Each individual is endowed with Free Will: the power to envision the possibilities, attracting one's most expansive reality. The present is our "escape hatch", our way out of limiting realities.

3. Like attracts like: what you deeply wish for yourself and others comes back to you.

4. There exists a *collective agreement* between all energies existing on the earth emphasizing certain beliefs and perceptions.

5. Beliefs create intention and realities are then attracted to that original intention.

6. We are divine, paradoxical beings possessing *Ego-Centered Consciousness and Soul (Core) Essence*. Infinite *Evolutionary Potentials:* vibrational probabilities are always available to attract.

7. Earth is the most important step in our evolution. It is on earth where we hone our attraction skills through understanding the role of beliefs and emotions and learning compassion.

8. No evil exists and we are eternal beings. Hence, there is no reason to fear.

9. The path is the goal: too much emphasis on reaching a prescribed goal can create a *"negative driving force"* (intention and attention).

10. Praying for others is the *"most powerful thing a person can do"*.

11. The God Force likes pleasure, likes to play.

12. We are made of sound and vibration: sound comes first in the universe.

13. Disputing traditional cause and effect karmic doctrine, Kuan Yin maintains that it is accumulated beliefs from parallel realities creating "made-up stories" about oneself and, thus, reality. Because of this quantum factor, we have absolute freedom to attract optimum realities from infinite, simultaneous Evolutionary Potentials. Thus, according to Kuan Yin, where and how skillfully one focuses their intention and attention can determine an outcome.

14. We are all divine beings having come to earth to gain potency through learning compassion and how to "liberate (spiritualize) matter", (Kuan Yin's euphemism for the law of energy transformation). Kuan Yin states, that what is missing on earth is "compassion for the untruth". "Compassion for the untruth", according to Kuan Yin, involves visualizing and affirming elements you believe can help resolve a given situation while remaining somewhat detached.

15. Motherly love, compassion and loving-kindness are the most potent forces in the universe.

16. Three limiting beliefs: the "not enough", "better than" and "survival of the fittest" form *"The Fear Triad"* and are responsible for much of the suffering on earth.

17. Militarism as well as environmental destruction primarily cannot occur without a belief in separation from each other and nature.

18. We are the jugglers of *"the dream and the world of dreams"* (this present reality and parallel realms).

19. No time exists. We've already lived "all of our lives".

20. The lesson on earth is acceptance of differences.

21. The state of divinity is defined by Kuan Yin as being in tune with nature as well as the acceptance of no past or future.

9
Loving Kindness

May 21, 2004: "Loving kindness is the most potent energy of all."
-Kuan Yin

During the previous week Lena had been reviewing some of her favorite books about Kuan Yin. Mentioning now, that one evening (after reading a few chapters chronicling one author's quest for anthropological data concerning Kuan Yin and also wondering about the progress of our book), she fell into a reverie. Somewhere between waking and sleeping Lena suddenly heard Kuan Yin say (in a loving and compassionate way), "You're trying to control something you can't. You'll know when the book is complete. However, in a very real sense, it is never really finished. It is, instead, an ongoing process."

"It's so interesting," continues Lena. "I never knew Kuan Yin was always encountered near bamboo, rocks and running water. I just always see her in that environment. And I don't exactly hear her words. It is as if my mind gets a concept: some kind of knowingness. Kuan Yin is like my steady rock, giver of everything non-material.

I continue to read how some Buddhist histories maintain Kuan Yin was once male. It is also believed that this male Kuan Yin was the deity originally worshipped by Buddhists."

"I'm feeling Kuan Yin very nearby," I mention to Lena. "There's a certain palpably-calming feeling when she's present. A warm, loving glow fills the room. I'm wondering if you will need to be counted down or if you're already there in the bamboo forest with Kuan Yin?"

"I feel her presence too. I'll need to be counted down though," replies Lena.

Reaching her "sacred place", experiencing a profound trance state, Lena begins to speak almost immediately:

"I see the waterfall, the bamboo forest. Kuan Yin has many arms this time. Seated on a silk blanket, her hands are holding many different things. She is showing me each arm in a three-dimensional way."

"Look at this arm!" commands Kuan Yin. "You've seen it in the book and now I'm showing it to you. So to attract and assist many people, I manifest in many ways. If it means being a man, it's fine with me. Whatever it takes! The world is about the different stages people are in."

"What about the pain my friends and I are experiencing about Iraq? Is there anything we can do? There is so much suffering and we don't seem to know how to change things.

Kuan Yin says that I'm too focused upon hopelessness," relays Lena. "It's interesting how Kuan Yin is pulling me along, from a cave-like place to a town square and now towards a bright light. Presently, it's as if I'm immersed in flower petals, but even softer.

She is holding my hand, pulling me further along. She wants me to go even higher and now is showing me something kind of interesting. Sometimes it takes me awhile to figure out the meaning of these journeys.

'Please help me understand, Kuan Yin. I don't have enough amplified senses. It is sometimes too detailed, too intricate.' I'll just visit with her for awhile and see if I can understand what she's trying to tell me."

"OK. Just tell me if you need anything," I reassure Lena.

"She's taking me deeper and deeper into a series of very smooth caves. I don't know what she wants me to do, to know. I'm asking her 'what is the right path to make the best use of my energy?'"

"There are places on the earth that are closer, more in keeping with my energies, than here, where you live," expounds Kuan Yin. "Materialism can take you further and further from your soul. There are places where one can feel closer to and rejuvenate one's spirit. While some have acquired many material things, they've lost something in the area of spirituality. Geographically, China is a place that holds elements of my energy. Don't only take into consideration the government [when determining the spiritual resonance of a particular region]. It can be regarded as a thin, paper veil, indeed a 'front-drop' for a greater energy. Mexico is another geographical location possessing a similar energy to mine. I feel sadness for your culture. Overly engrossed, *invested* in the birth, death cycle, many don't understand that most naturally-occurring 'circumstances' regarding the above are attracted at a soul vibration level."

"I've wondered why I sometimes feel pulled to visit India," confesses Lena.

"You could go there. It is a place to strengthen oneself in a consistent way. Keep communicating with me and I'll arrange for you to visit a power spot on the earth."

"I was consciously aware when I was very young," continues Lena. "I knew I had been separated from somewhere, *someone*. It was like being intensely homesick. I was terribly sad and lonely all the time."

"A lot of spirit energies are 'coming in' all the time. Soul evolution is linear for some, non-linear for others. Some jump around experiencing a variety of lifetimes. It's a way for the soul to develop compassion," informs Kuan Yin.

"I've always wondered if I was being punished; whether the punishment involved re-experiencing struggle on the earth," ponders Lena, from her trance. "Now I'm starting to remember what happened: Other beings are telling me that I was a different kind of a being, involved in helping people from a distance. Back then, I felt trapped in a body. But I see now how I wanted to do this, to separate from the group. I'd spent too much time there, with them. 'You were very courageous,' I hear them, the beings, say to me. Wow. I'm seeing myself comment:

'Look at how they, the earth energies, suffer; how they die. Emerging from even the most tragic death, their energy still keeps on going. What is it like to die, to feel pain?'

I guess I believed I wouldn't be *real* unless I experienced being human. Furthermore, I couldn't seem to stand my own curiosity.

'You were very brave,' I again hear the beings (who I'd been with), say. 'Don't get sucked-in! Don't fall off that cliff; that suffering state of mind,' they had warned me. They didn't want me to get caught up in the suffering of others," remarks Lena after a moment's pause: 'Why did you want to go? We didn't want you to go. If you decide to leave and experience earth you'll know more than us!'

I was a part of that family and I wandered off. They are telling me, now, that there really are demigods waiting in line to be born, to manifest as humans. In this way, they can evolve faster. It is apparently so; that we come to earth to further evolve."

"This time I took you through the 'back door', the place where 'energies' (I don't refer to energies in a hierarchical fashion—as 'higher or 'lower'), come into human form." continues Kuan Yin. "They evolve from a different *angle:* down to up, with not much of a 'past'. Others have more experience. The confusion on earth is created by a variety of different energies. Any clash between energies is a result of a *better than* mindset. Sometimes the children are even dragged into this mindset and then there are awful consequences. What people need to remember is they are eternal beings and that they never die.

However, don't let these events distract you from reality. Reality is always truth, knowledge and bliss.

Sometimes things are none of our business. A playground fight is a perfect example. Those participating in the fight have an agreement. One can stand back and watch and maybe even offer comfort. Those engaged in the fight however, don't have to accept one's compassionate offer. One of your lessons, Lena, is detachment. Don't become addicted to negative news. There are some who want to be in a negative space, misusing doctrines."

"Kuan Yin's knee is up similar to some of the pictures I've seen of her," describes Lena. "She's very assertive right now, in her power mode:"

"I'm not going to force anything on them. They have free will. Free will," Kuan Yin reiterates.

"But they're subjecting *us* to their ugliness, *their* drama," objects Lena.

"Well, sure. You do what you can, Lena. There are so many realities. This is a microcosm of the whole, just one reality. From your vantage point it appears cruel and inhuman."

"Aren't we supposed to be helping them? What can we do?" inquires Lena.

"Don't pass along the beliefs and actions you disapprove of to your children. Loving-kindness is potent even when displayed during the so-called mundane tasks of daily existence. It's so potent that if everyone could get into that mindset for a minute or even less, they would blast into a great ball of light. Even the newest (smallest) energies would blast through," emphasizes Kuan Yin.

"I'm experiencing a thick and heavy *karmic fog*, globs of hate, revenge and murder," portrays Lena. "Kuan Yin is demonstrating how powerful loving kindness can be: that it can disintegrate even this, the darkest of energies."

"As children mostly do not judge nor intend harm, loving kindness is always easier to express to them," acknowledges Kuan Yin. "Learning from these experiences, one can begin to treat everyone as they would a child. After all, the only real thing one can do is to love and be loved. As I've said before, mother's love is the closest to loving-kindness. Teach my message. *Practice* my message."

"I wish I could do all of this in my daily life," laments Lena."

"Gain strength. Suck up energy. Make a point of appreciating the fragrance of the flowers and the beauty of the sunset. It is like armor. When you take a moment to practice my message you can then be armed with an ability to be detached. One is meant to forgive, to forgive and be compassionate. Raise your voice in protest, while maintaining your detachment."

"Kuan Yin is leading me back. She says we're complete for today."

Commentary: More Love, More Joy!

The more you are able to bring into focus those elements in your life that bring you fulfillment, the more love and joy you can attract into your reality. This is the Goddess's profound message.

Kuan Yin has emphasized the importance of a specific kind of focus—*focused intent*: its role in the attraction of reality. You may have already discovered that various thoughts and feelings have their unique vibrations. Having their particular quality and intensity, your thoughts and intentions ripple out and reecho back, penetrating everything in your physical and non-physical worlds.

Contrary to certain belief systems; we have not incarnated into these unique and complex bodies to learn how to *lose* our individuality. Nor are we meant to rescind our power. An essential cornerstone of Kuan Yin's canons is that a *realistic life* allows one to better realize their infinite potential. The more that we are able to develop ingenuity along with choosing harmonious reality-parameters to focus upon the happier we tend to be. Such profound inner peace is success in life. The more one is in harmony with themselves: the more harmony one can create in the universe.

Examples of how visions, thoughts and emotions are the building blocks of countless realities; Kuan Yin's parables and metamorphisms show evolutions proceeding from the original thought form. A possible envisioning could include regarding one's life as their ever-malleable personal creation and repeating: "I see myself beginning and pursuing each day with joy: only attracting those circumstances aligned with my highest goals." To make your personally inspired Evolutionary Potential a 'vibrational fit', embellish it with complimentary soaring emotions.

Kuan Yin states that the universe will bring "whatever one wants". Happiness should always be considered a relative term. Whether instant or long term: gratification and happiness must ultimately match one's deepest sensibilities, wherever one is on that spectrum. Upon this happiness foundation we are already in abundance. Aware of one's innate power, one can call forth from the depths of one's very Core, the self-sustaining manna. We can decide the direction for the road ahead. And then, brick by brick; build that road.

10
Kuan Yin with A Thousand Arms

May 27, 2004: "Don't forget to marvel at the wonders of the world."
-*Kuan Yin*

Having had a particularly stressful week, Lena wondered whether Kuan Yin would appear to her again:

"I feel so frustrated with my life. Last week I felt so far away from Kuan Yin's teachings, so angry and stressed. Everything feels so unjust. It's as if my therapist doesn't even hear me.

But I felt Kuan Yin this morning in my heart. During my massage, I saw her. She was immense, having thousands of arms. In each hand is a symbol, tools for understanding our lives. She was grasping different things like a candle, the Buddha, hands with eyes, a lotus, the Buddhist symbol for peace, her bottle containing healing elixir; instruments which are for peacefully slaying injustice, the fog of indecision. These are instruments for one's protection, as well.

I've been trying to practice compassion," Lena continues. "I recall Kuan Yin saying to me that there is a time and place for compassion."

"Are you comfortable? Are you ready to be counted down?"

"Yes."

"Do you need a longer countdown? Or is the standard ten to zero ok for today?"

"The standard one will probably be fine for today."

After experiencing the standard leading, pacing and then a countdown from ten to zero, Lena found herself, once again, in the peaceful Bamboo grove with the waterfall:

"Kuan Yin is here, now. She is immense, having many arms, many *dimensions*. She's so real. I'm amazed by the realness of her flesh. I get the impression that she needs to come to me right now. She knows how difficult this week has been for me, my emotions and my physical pain."

"I've been close by you, lately," Kuan Yin comforts Lena. "I want to stay near to you to help and to show you strength. Sometimes it's ok to go inside and work on your own personal issues rather than being so concerned about the outside realm. You know that I can't interfere with karma. The karmic cycle is just.

However, one can ride karma like a wave. I have the tools and everyone can choose to utilize them to improve their lives. Sometimes the waves are small. Sometimes the waves are big. In order to help others, one must learn how to help oneself."

"Should I use mantras? Ritual?" inquires Lena.

"You don't have to," answers Kuan Yin, speaking lovingly to Lena. "I'll come to you in any form. Respect the Masters: those who've passed down tools for enlightenment. If the rituals don't help, you don't need to do them. Mantras and ritual won't bring you any closer to me than the kind of exchange we are experiencing right now."

"Dealing with people sometimes seems so challenging," remarks Lena. "How can I be fair and not judge others?"

"Constant 'checking-in', constant inner reflection," replies Kuan Yin. "It's not always going to be fair. Human nature isn't always fair. The main challenge is how to handle daily issues and still not hurt others. Always be reflective. Be honest and have integrity. One can utilize the divine tools, similar to the one's I am holding in my hands, and still maintain one's human nature. I want to discuss the mistakes and inaccuracies of human existence. Human existence and human tendencies are wrapped in karma."

"My arm is really hurting, at the moment." Lena mentions, from deep within her trance.

"Do you want to rest for a moment?" I ask.

"I think so."

Repositioning her arm into a more comfortable position, Lena continues to speak:

"I'm trying to understand what Kuan Yin is saying, here. I think she's saying human mistakes and inaccuracies are no less important than divinity. The human condition creates divinity in the higher self. Thus, it is very important to be human and not to shun or hate our humanity. The incredible process of being human allows for the higher self to acknowledge and extract divinity from one's trials and tribulations.

Now I'm seeing the face of a guru I once knew. I'm seeing it over and over."

"He hated his humanity," intervenes Kuan Yin. "Such hatred is not helpful at all. In fact, it's unnatural. And it is really not the truth. The truth is one must be fully human for the divine part of self to be more in tune. Rejecting the human body assures one will have to come back, return to the lessons here on earth. It means 'you didn't get it'," counsels Kuan Yin.

"Many contemporary religions don't 'get it'. The indigenous tribes are the most powerful as many of them are so in harmony with nature as to be really, really divinely human. They're so in touch with their humanity that they're totally in tune with their Diva nature. They know that human/nature harmony is the crux of spirituality.

Of course there is always the criticism: that "better than" mindset. Humans say they're better than each other. And they say they're better than nature. But they're not. It's ludicrous to compare the intelligence of other living creatures to human intelligence. Plants have enormous intelligences and spirituality. However, the "better than" mindset greatly contributes to the ongoing environmental destruction.

The earth is trying to teach humans that everything is spirit. Eventually, humans will learn. It's just another way to understand divinity. Spirit works through one's own humanity and the earth. Everything here (on earth) is for the divine evolution of *all* energies. Whereas the word 'beings' so often refers only to humans, I use the term *energies* as it encompasses all living things on the planet."

"I'm just watching Kuan Yin, her amazement of creation," notes Lena. "But why, Kuan Yin, is it so difficult to deal with people?"

"You can't change people. You can love them and give to them. If they can't receive, it's not a reason not to love them. Do your best. However, don't fall into the trap of expecting a reward for doing good deeds. Do a good deed because it is the right thing to do.

Look at Christ, the saints. Jesus came with a message. Much of humanity is still feeling sorry for him. He's not feeling sorry for himself," recounts Kuan Yin. "It is important to accept that the human condition is temporary, fleeting. It's filled with pain and suffering, beauty, strange tastes, odors of death, *everything* that exists in the universe.

Problems can be created when one is so obsessed with his or her own death, when one is too attached to their life. This attachment to a single incarnation causes the species to play out gruesome deaths. If humans knew they were more than just this life, they would not plunder the land, each other.

Death is like giving birth. Birth can be painful. Sometimes women die from giving birth. However, once the baby is born, all the pain vanishes in an instant. Love for that tiny newborn makes one forget the pain, the fear. And as I've said before: love between mother and child is the highest experience, the closest to divine love.

You might wonder about the parallel I'm making between birth and death. But I say to you, the fear and pain accompanying an awful death is over quickly. Beyond that portal one is suddenly in the light, in oneness and bliss.

Some women are powerful teachers. However, even women can be afraid of death, forget how the pain vanishes. Just as a woman heals rapidly after childbirth and then is able to fall in love with her baby, those who pass over also are able to fall in love with a new life."

"Should I change myself if I'm not able to change others?" Lena asks.

"I come from a realm where there is instant, mind to mind understanding. There can be no lies, no misunderstanding. Conversely, in this realm humans have to work very hard to be understood. They must be able to clearly communicate verbally and/or through writing. The human body and its communication tools are heavy and cumbersome compared to my realm. One has to be very clear and perhaps even write things down. Work hard to make things clear and then review what you've learned."

"It seems difficult," responds Lena.

"Well, that's what you have to do. If you're not clear, how can you expect others to be clear?"

"We're in such complicated human forms," notes Lena.

"Don't forget to marvel at the wonders of the world." reminds Kuan Yin.

"Oh wow." exclaims Lena. "I'm seeing so many beautiful things. I see a flower. Oh, now a lizard. A bumblebee. Unseen things! Energies. Plants! Raindrops!"

"Remember to marvel at these things when you've had enough, for the time being, of the human realm. Science helps one marvel. Scientists might not think of themselves as being spiritual. However, the knowledge they bring to the world is very spiritual.

Remember the time you told your daughter how astonishing kangaroos are? You told her how the tiny baby kangaroo crawls out of the mother kangaroo's vagina and up into her pouch even as the mother is still bouncing," reminds Kuan Yin.

"I did tell my daughter that, didn't I?" marvels Lena at Kuan Yin's accuracy concerning the details of her waking life.

"There are marvels under the sea. There are great examples in nature of how to behave, live in harmony. However humans don't necessarily follow their example. Observe, for example, the geese, how they stay in perfect chevron formation; perfect cooperation while flying towards their destination."

Kuan Yin continues: "You might find it helpful to read about the many tools I hold in my hands. I can tell you they are often metaphors for human qualities and also tools humans can use to balance their lives. Once in balance, one is in harmony with the universe.

Try to keep yourself in balance and then you will be in harmony when dealing with your karma. Take some time alone to rejuvenate. Maybe a little time away from your family, an overnight stay might be useful. Whatever feeds your strength," encourages Kuan Yin.

"What about feeling guilty?" Lena asks abruptly.

"Guilt is not a very productive mood. One of the things I hold in my hand can be utilized to alleviate guilt. However, don't rely on other culture's symbols and interpretations. They might not work for you. Focus on whatever positive trait you want to achieve, almost like you would focus on a musical note. Fashion your own personal symbols and interpretations, those that work for you. Peace be with you and Hope.

I'm with you, Hope, as much as I'm with Lena. I look forward to an eternal connection with you. Always remember me. *Come* to me."

"She's leaving us a beautiful lotus to remember her by," explains Lena. "And as she bids us goodbye, she repeats once again, 'remember to marvel'."

Commentary: Remember to Marvel!

Marveling, according to Kuan Yin, is an empathetic act, wherein one actually opens to, melds with and consequently *alters* the object being marveled at. Indeed, as this is a reciprocal relationship, the one who marvels will likely also be profoundly changed. Paramount to the marveling process is the development of a specific kind of focus: perceiving a given object in a deep and personal way. Genuine marveling ultimately requires that one fully *be* with the object. One can then *"think oneself there"*, moving in change and appreciating that which is also observed. Momentarily liberated from time and space, one may quite effortlessly encounter one's own divinity.

An essential purpose of Kuan Yin's shape shifting is to remind us of the boundlessness of the human spirit; that behind all physical manifestation is the rock solid bulwark of our beliefs and their resulting resonance. She wants us to know that all matter whether animate or inanimate, visible or invisible is alive and that acts of marveling and compassion are integral to the *spiritualization of matter.*

The challenge for humanity, then, is to balance the artificial time scaffolding of ego-centered consciousness with effective focused intent: when and where your place your attention. Regard time and space as a sacred gift: a temporary anchor within an ever-shifting universe. Skillfully managing these can lead to empowerment. Such a vibrant focus is suddenly a powerfully magnetizing force that can nurture and sustain you.

This is the profound power of marveling and being grateful for one's life. Therefore, embellish your life with broad and colorful brushstrokes. Marvel at the kindness of strangers. Marvel at the wondrous creations of mankind. Marvel at the sunrise and sunset. And marvel at your own ability to marvel.

And when totally engaged in your blissful state, don't forget to marvel at your humanity: how you have infinite power to love and receive all the bounties the universe has to offer.

11
The Good & Pious Warriors

June 3, 2004: "Kuan Yin wants to help the good and pious warriors. She says sometimes the words, "good" and "pious" can mean "afraid of pain": that those energies staying away from the real challenges are more afraid of pain then of loving God."
-*Kuan Yin*

A few days before my weekly scheduled meeting with Lena, I experienced a dream relating to a topic that had surfaced during a previous Kuan Yin session: one's silver umbilical cord. Falling asleep early that particular evening, I'd felt out of sorts all night.

Encountering Kuan Yin, I was ecstatic to be with her in my dreams. Instructing that I could heal certain issues by 'fine-tuning' the color and tone of my silver umbilical cord, she pointed to a segment of my own cord. Not the healthy color I expected, to my astonishment it looked somewhat dark and withered.

Expanding upon her technique for fine-tuning the silver umbilical cord to a healthy and vibrant color, she assured me that incorporating such visualizations could have a positive effect. Together in the dream we were able to visualize my spiritual umbilical cord as a vibrant silvery tone. I awoke from this very informative dream feeling much better.

Trying this technique again in my waking state, I found it to be very helpful.

Discussing other matters at the beginning of this particular trance session, I overlooked telling Lena about my dream. Interestingly, in spite of my omission, Kuan Yin describes her expertise in healing early in the discourse.

Exhausted and in much pain, Lena mentions (before being counted down) how in the past, a therapist had once commented on Lena's hunched-over posture: how it represented a desire to protect her heart:

"I know of the anger and rage that comes right through a blow and into your heart. Your heart gets broken over and over. Very often, I can feel people's pain, those here in the US and in other countries. I felt my brothers' pain during the times they were also being abused by my father. But, I want to let go of the pain Hope, not *own* it anymore."

"I've learned through the years that one must sometimes be vigilant in one's efforts to cultivate, actually re-envision new and positive thoughts and images when recalling one's 'past'. And as we live in a quantum-universe, I suppose it's reasonable to assume that future decisions can actually alter the past. Are you ready to go into trance, now?"

"Yes."

Returning to her sacred bamboo garden, Lena describes what she is presently witnessing:

"Yes I'm here. I'm very tiny, cradled by Kuan Yin's palms. They are so big; it's as if she is holding her bottle of elixir. However, it is *me* she is holding in the curved areas of her hands."

"I bet you didn't think you'd end up here?" Kuan Yin gently teases. "I know that you're not feeling well, physically or emotionally. There have been so many shocks to your system. You need a lot of rest. Your body wants to rest. Try to make the time for it."

"Kuan Yin is very happy to see me even though I'm feeling weak and discouraged. It's as if she was my grandmother and I was coming home from school not feeling well. Wise and comforting, she pats me on the head and assures me I'll be ok. I'm telling her my solar plexus feels so tired, drained, not nurtured. Does she know of any herbs?"

"My specialty is healing," Kuan Yin reassures. "I come to each person in a different form. Sometimes, I will come even in the crudest of forms if it leads people to their rightful path. I provide whatever one's soul wants, whatever one is ready for or evolved to.

It's very difficult to keep certain beings on this planet. For those who've come from higher planes and had access to other, more heightened senses, experiences here can make the earth feel like a prison. It was difficult to keep Lena here. She was always trying to reject her body.

You Lena, immediately regretted coming to earth. In fact, you had tried to minimize the illusion of this planet, beforehand: before you fully incarnated here. You were worried you would forget how to get back 'home' to your planet of origin. Add to this, the fact that you didn't realize the force, the *heaviness* of coming through the layers and down to the earth plane!

You panicked. You didn't want to merge too much with this reality and forget your real home. At the same time, you didn't want to return home. Your desires to go back home and to stay here and help, learn compassion were in direct conflict. To always remember your place of origin, you believed you would require some constant reminder, some kind of an abusive situation to keep you yearning for home.

You finally came across a family that met your criteria. You *chose*, then, a family that would not destroy you, but would, however, significantly wound you. You are, in some ways, still *stuck* in that abusive childhood situation. Earth is a place where one has to be strong, (persisting on in their lives, even in the midst of difficulty). Lena is strong."

"Kuan Yin is telling me I'm strong even though I'm feeling very weak," admits Lena. "Kuan Yin wants to find people like me and you, Hope who went *downward* in their karmic cycle; who are 'lower' than they were before."

"Pious doesn't mean one has completed their karma," stresses Kuan Yin. "Not until one has experienced the 'darkness' (which is really ignorance), is one spiritually complete. Ignorance is a term often used to refer to those who are convinced of something that is not truth. It also can refer to investment in a certain, limiting identity.

One can be pious and good however not necessarily a *warrior*. Some of those remaining in the 'loftier' realms are fearful of being with other's pain. It is too scary for them."

"Kuan Yin wants to help the good and pious warriors. She says sometimes the words 'good' and 'pious' can mean 'afraid of pain': that those energies staying away from the real challenges are more afraid of pain then of loving God." concludes Lena.

"Much of the strength you, Lena, possess comes from faith that everything happens for a reason," emphasizes Kuan Yin "However, it takes a lot of strength to have faith. The illusion of earth can be a distraction. *Maya* is amazingly seductive. It can make one think he or she is bigger than the cosmos, and dissolve everything you've spiritually worked for.

All are equal in value. However, some don't always express themselves constructively. Sometimes they even bring other's down with their words. No one's more special than anyone else."

"Why am I able to have such a good connection with you, Kuan Yin? Is there some special karmic connection?" wonders Lena.

"Oh yes. On the earth plane, long ago." responds Kuan Yin "You worshipped my image many times. For your energy, your karmic path, I'm your greatest connection."

"She became very attached to me," continues Lena; comprehending her former relationship with Kuan Yin. "She *looked out* for me. Some are assigned to a deity. I am. And it means that my energy force is congruent with the way Kuan Yin is expressed in the world. As humans, though, we're really even beyond that identity. Nirvana, the path to finding Oneness, can be obtained when identifying with Kuan Yin. However, it is impossible to have only one deity. We all have many deities, as we need their different qualities, *energies* in order to reach Oneness, the point of no identity. Wow. One can really get misled from false teachers," exclaims Lena, suddenly spying a group of misled souls.

"Kuan Yin is reminding me to embrace my humanity. I'm telling her how much pain I'm in, how I just want to be free to do my work."

"It won't always be this discouraging," consoles Kuan Yin "I'll send hints on what can be helpful to your body, such as herbs, etc. These suggestions will come from people and places you are familiar with. Be aware and take advantage of the opportunities that will come your way next week."

"I guess I got lonely for Kuan Yin's geographical power centers such as China and Mexico. She tells me I'd benefit from the "collective agreement" or *"collective energy"* that can be felt in these places. The potency of such energy could help me feel better about my life," concludes Lena.

"She tells me there are a lot of places that hold Her energy. But she is going to end now, she doesn't want me to overdo."

"You're ready now to be counted back up?"

"Yes."

Stretching, coming fully into her waking state of consciousness after being counted up from her sacred place, Lena mentioned something very interesting:

"Hope, when she mentions you during our talks together, she's always over by your side. She told me she's always with you and she wants you to be aware of her messages. Trust in your relationship with her, her guidance."

Commentary: A Vision of Sustainable Technology on Earth

Thoughts and their accompanying emotions, according to Kuan Yin, create varying probable imprints for personal and mass realities. A particular outcome will depend upon consistent or contrasting elements contained in such imprints. Intimately associated with molecular process theories, the building up and breaking down of these imprints create uncountable parallel universes.

Demonstrating this, Kuan Yin's metamorphisms show evolutions proceeding from the origin imprint. Naturally, when learning to navigate the "grand plan", there can be distortions: limiting belief systems spiraling whole civilizations into chaos.

Separate from this, there are even those among us professing that dwelling just beneath the very soil we daily tread upon and which so magnificently sustains us, live the malevolent spirits of hell. Perhaps such a belief is the original inspiration for certain ambivalent and even hostile attitudes towards stewardship of the earth. Or is simply the notion that mankind has primacy over all of nature? Indeed, any "untruth" could continue to attract limiting realities.

According to Kuan Yin, it is the above self-perpetuating dynamic inflating the present Evolutionary Potential. There exist, in parallel universes, both sustainable and non-sustainable technological EP's. It is possible to attract and implement concepts for a more efficient, environmentally-sustainable reality; but only once the majority of humanity is in agreement.

We have finally adopted a more holistic approach. Embracing earth sustainability represents a sea change for a culture once chronically suspicious of the natural world. There have been admirable breakthroughs in contemporary scientific/technological disciplines. Adopting a truly objective overview allows us to comprehend humanity as innately compassionate and nature as its exquisitely harmonious and co-operative counterpart.

Civilization is presently faced with clear alternatives. Standing at this very serious precipice, we absolutely must focus our collective attention towards healing the earth and her children. One can begin this process by learning to effectively attract (on a personal level) one's greatest potentials.

Implementing the positive beliefs and values that define our humanity can result in directing resources and technology towards peaceful coexistence and restoration of the ecosphere. Right now, we have the power to imagine the benefits when the billions of dollars devoted to war are applied to humanitarian and environmental efforts.

Many have already espoused that both personal and mass problems we face today are fundamentally philosophical. One can pass laws, but unless addressing the philosophical core, the promise of achieving a peaceful and bountiful Evolutionary Potential, may continue to elude us.

12
The Most Divine Life Imaginable

June 10, 2004: "The best thing you can do is to get on the path. No. Let me restate that. Keep it your goal—the *path of liberation*. If you try to force the image or path you can lose your taste for it…No two paths look the same."
-*Kuan Yin*

Meeting at our regular scheduled time, Lena and I prepare for our afternoon session together. Mentioning a little earlier that she had gone to the local bookstore during the week, to see if she was attracted to any of the books on the shelves, she seemed disappointed:

"It felt so heavy in there, like everyone was almost too intent on finding truth. I went away quite disillusioned, not buying anything."

Eventually finding a comfortable position, Lena also mentions that she'd been having more difficulty than usual with the pain in her shoulder. Deciding it might be beneficial to just before beginning the actual countdown to her sacred place, to experience certain hypnotic pain management techniques, Lena is also experiencing some discomfort in her stomach, today.

I wait for Lena to lay back and relax. Making the hypnotic suggestion that she breathe out the pain into the earth, (and then transform it into something beneficial for the earth) I then direct her to breathe in healing energy into both her shoulder and solar plexus areas.

Feeling somewhat better, Lena advises me she is ready to begin the actual countdown. Having the intention of reaching first her "safe place" and then her "sacred place", we proceed with our standard trance protocol.

Quite different from her usual sacred place with the bamboo forest and waterfall, Lena finds herself standing on a shoreline somewhere in the Eastern hemisphere of the world: she believes perhaps in Eastern China:

"Yes," Lena murmurs, "I'm standing on a beach. Everything seems so real. I don't see a lot of sand. Instead, I'm seeing profoundly beautiful round stones stretching as far as the eye can see. I see Kuan Yin. She is like Venus, statuesque and standing in front of a beautiful pink half-shell. Quickly, she walks in front of me, pointing the way.

We are entering the mouth of a cave. It's so interesting. I see stairs carved out of rock in the cave. We walk up the stairs to a door. I know somehow this is just another entrance, a doorway to another time, place. Perhaps at another historical time monks lived there. Now, I'm seeing a huge image; a beautiful statue of Kuan Yin at the very top of the mountain. There are stairs leading up to her. It is as if I'm right on location, standing alongside a group of worshippers.

I feel the potency of her energy. In these places, perhaps China or Vietnam, there is a palpable sense of being immersed in and supported by her presence. There is a need by the people to know more, to pick up and accumulate wisdom.

I'm suddenly feeling a need to be in that kind of energy. However, it's not an intellectual kind of need. It's a bit different from the more male-impacted Buddhism."

Suddenly it is Kuan Yin who is speaking:

"Some believe I am in servitude to Buddha. However, Buddha doesn't see it like that. We're more like brother and sister. I'm showing, Lena, my abode, a place on earth where humans can visit me and be in my potency. Lena is looking at my statue and then at my form. There's a difference.

I come to people in many forms, forms constructed from people's own *perceptions* of how I should come to them. And it is individual spiritual needs that create these unique perceptions. In the end, it does not matter what form I take."

"Kuan Yin wants me to know that I can have the most divine life imaginable," whispers Lena, still very deep in trance. "She'll be here until the last soul passes off the earth. She remains in deity form to assist people in transcending their materialistic nature, to help them attain their highest spiritual level. She's not angry. She's just a little impatient in wanting me to keep up with her.

However, she's relaxed, casual. I don't sense any punishment energy. She treats me like a friend: 'How can I help? What is it you want me to know Kuan Yin?'"

"The best thing you can do is to get on the path. No. Let me restate that. Keep it your goal: the *path of liberation*. If you try to force the image or path you can lose your taste for it."

"Kuan Yin is warning me not to do too much reading on the subject. Sometimes the ancient monks' writings were specifically related to a particular monk or times."

When several monks wrote together, they formed books not necessarily related to *your* path. No two paths look the same," maintains Kuan Yin.

Further describing her experience at the bookstore, Lena continues:

"Now I know why I had that feeling at the bookstore. The stagnation! The heaviness: People desperately searching for knowledge!"

"Tradition is good," Kuan Yin acknowledges. "However, in the Western Culture there are so many people looking for wisdom. It is important to get familiar with the various paths. Such a process develops character for one to look inward for their right path. People who've never suffered haven't yet developed an ability to utilize their own creativity to solve a challenging situation. An analogy would be that of a person who has fallen into a well:

After many attempts of trying to climb out, they develop strength, ingenuity. That is what many are doing on this earth. However, devastating struggle is always karmic. It might seem karmic if one has had a bad day or week. However, 'little suffering' is for the purpose of building character and inner trust. On the other hand, extreme suffering for no apparent reason is an indication one is dealing with big karma.

One usually finds a deity or god, who can help liberate, teach them. It is not helpful, however, to have a deity *forced* upon one. It may be the wrong angel or the wrong guide. In such a case, the guide (or religion) can have the effect of having the individual not perceive *anything* spiritual or cause them to believe they've failed. Unfortunately, sometimes in these instances, individuals will shun their own spiritual path.

I don't have to warn Hope. However, Lena is drawn to philosophy. And sometimes because of its dryness, delving too deeply into philosophy can block out the heart."

"I'm recalling a Buddhist parable," says Lena. "It involves an individual who climbs the mountain to receive wisdom from a monk. If one comes to the monk with an empty container, that individual can be filled with wisdom. On the other hand, if one comes filled with preconceptions; one's mind already made up, any new knowledge or wisdom will simply spill over."

"Yes." agrees Kuan Yin. "The best state of meditation is to come to these sessions with an 'empty cup'. Then you can receive new information without any forced structure or chronology. Hope knows that. The Seth Books are congruent with my teachings. Hope learned not to 'jam her cup' with too much intellectualism. It closes off the heart. Think of the head as the top of the bottle. If it is too tightly, firmly 'screwed on', it closes off the entire *vessel*.

The message, then, is to not *lose your head*. If the head is 'lost', true wisdom, knowledge cannot reach the heart."

"Kuan Yin is also warning me not to read too much Zen Buddhism," relays Lena. I got a glimpse of this message while I was getting a massage earlier this week. Kuan Yin was there with me during my weekly therapeutic massage. She was telling me that knowledge, particularly the history of Kuan Yin, could be more authentically assimilated if it is a slow process. I need to, also visit the places where her energy is potent."

"The knowledge of the everyday people is more realistic," contends Kuan Yin. "Being a monk is not very realistic. As a mother, Lena has an opportunity to live a 'realistic life'. One can, then, achieve important goals without renouncing everything. Those who are committed to me: family people: a family fisherwoman and fisherman, for example, as well as all the humble villagers, are very dear to my heart.

No one is better than someone else. Monks are no more spiritual, for instance, than a humble villager. I want this to be taught to my devout followers. I suffer from my followers' beliefs that they are unworthy of me. This is why we are here in the fishing village, today. There are those who feel guilty because they could not send their son or daughter to be a monk, that their children were desperately needed at home to help support the family.

I feel sad about their guilt. They need not feel guilty. Those who do sacrifice their sons or daughters as monks also miss the fact that both occupations; fisherman and monk, are equal."

"I want to ask Kuan Yin if I can help her pray for the villagers. I'm now sending prayers to Kuan Yin's loyal devotees; that they understand and awaken to the fact that their devotion is just as powerful as that of a monk. Kuan Yin is telling me our exchange is over for today."

"Are you ready, then, to return, to be counted back up?"

"Yes."

When Lena returned to her waking state she commented upon how everything was so real during her trance, especially the stunning three-dimensional beauty of the stones and pebbles on the beach. Then she mentioned how she'd left a rose for Kuan Yin before returning to waking state.

Commentary: Utilizing Imagination and Creativity to Solve a Challenging Situation

Kuan Yin states that many individuals have come to the earth to acquire "strength and ingenuity" through utilizing imagination and creativity to solve a challenging situation; that learning focus, ingenuity and compassion is the path to liberation.

Stating: *"You can have a hope. However, to agonize over the future is not very skillful,"* Kuan Yin explains that worry and other inhibiting thought projections are most definitely not the purpose of imagination. With these amazing minds of ours, we are meant to imagine the most expansive possibilities. Any other kind of imagining could result in distortion. It is because the earth offers us diverse and endless opportunities to fully explore, indeed *test the waters* that Kuan Yin stresses it is this present; this "realistic life" that is our opportunity for self-realization.

According to the Goddess, the greatest reward will never alone be materialistic wealth. At some point during the process of becoming, we simply appreciate the miracle of who we are. It is this appreciation that leads us to one of our main purposes here on earth, to be the masters of our own destiny.

Before our entrance into the world, there was our resonance: those unique vibrations springing from one's most deeply held beliefs. Resonance is just one of the seven innate forces influencing our lives. The following lists all seven: beliefs, free will, emotions, vibration (tonal resonance), imagination, intuition and creativity. It's important to remember that these forces are synergistic: that they are more than the sum of their parts.

What one believes, for example, will intimately affect one's emotions, vibration, imagination and intention.

What we want to create in our lives is the 'dream' of lasting joy and fulfillment. One can have nightly dreams that are expansive or limiting.

Some of them are pleasing and some can be overwhelming. Kuan Yin's Law of Compassion is always our waking reflection: whether or not we are actualizing a true Kuan Yin State of Grace. The essence of that vision can be so ephemeral. The way to actualize that fragile vision is to draw it in as physical reality.

No matter how correct you believe yourself to be, Kuan Yin suggests practicing what she terms "detached compassion" towards even the most contrary view points and actions. This involves being able to envision and give energy to the most beneficial outcome while remaining detached. Mastery of this, Kuan Yin's "Compassion for the Untruth" is important as it can create an inner calm capable of attracting other enlightening experiences to you.

13
Living the Dream

June 24, 2004: "You're at page ten but I understand the entire evolution. In reality, it's already over. It's a dream. Remember? You're living a dream. It's very complicated to hold the dream and live the dream. You are learning the art of juggling the dream and the world of dreams. Nobody really gets hurt."
-*Kuan Yin*

Her surgery date quickly approaching (in mid-July), Lena and I agreed before beginning the session, that it might be helpful (if during the countdown) we were to pre-observe the circumstances surrounding her scheduled surgery.

So, at the number five, I employed the leading and pacing verbiage allowing for a psychic detour, an opportunity for Lena to preview the operating room environment where her surgery will take place. Immediately and methodically, Lena begins describing what she is witnessing:

"Everyone is wearing white. I can hear them talking to each other. As this is a teaching college, everyone is watching and learning. They may even be filming the entire surgery. I see the orthopedic surgeon, the concern on his face. He is being extremely careful, noting the precise placement of the muscles, veins and arteries near my left shoulder. I can see all these components myself, how they are so complex. All seems to be going very smoothly. There is a very cerebral atmosphere. Each participant is very interested in the procedure and its outcome."

Having completed the preview of her upcoming surgery, Lena was then ready to be fully counted down to her sacred place. Continuing on, I counted Lena down to the number 0, suggesting she discover her sacred place:

"It's interesting," comments Lena, elaborating upon what she had experienced during today's countdown. "During the countdown I saw a vision of a little cabin on a lake. Sitting on the back porch of the cabin, I glimpsed the groundskeeper, a chubby and elderly sage. Maybe it was

Buddha; maybe Kuan Yin. I'm not sure. Whoever it was, they were a person of great mystery and wonder. Now I see lots of water. A lake! Waterfalls: misty, surreal waterfalls. Kuan Yin is at once the waterfall and *in* the waterfall. Now, her dress *is* the waterfall. She is very young and beautiful.

Kuan Yin is showing me a dolphin in the ocean. I can see through the layers of her dress, as if it were a screen. The dolphin is leaping through the screen, now. She is showing me the beauty of the different animals.

Let me just sit with Kuan Yin for a moment and try to comprehend. I wish I could ask her where one can go, in this country, to experience the wonderful atmosphere created wherever she is worshipped. The reason I would like to discover such a place is that I believe there is more that I'm supposed to learn."

"You don't have to follow Buddhist scriptures," begins Kuan Yin. "Just see my image, *create* my image. Understand all my manifestations. Watch my pastimes! They like to see me riding a dragon. So, I get to ride a dragon," she laughs. "Sometimes, they like to envision me as a man," she laughs again.

"Kuan Yin is very playful, today," notes Lena.

"Feel free to look through all the books and texts. Maybe something will capture your fancy. You've seen my image in your dreams," Kuan Yin remarks happily while playfully shape-shifting.

"She knows how I love little babies," explains Lena. "So, she's perched there on a low branch holding an infant in her arms. Now she's shape shifting again. I'm asking her how to help the people of the world. I understand that there is karma but I feel so connected to everyone, even the suffering. She's pulling me along. We're flying high above Iraq, Saudi Arabia.

'Please protect these people,'" I implore Kuan Yin. "I have so much grief about the war. I want Kuan Yin to create a miracle, to change hearts and minds. Stop the killing!

Wow! She just tore the countries right off the map. Suddenly, she's wrapping them tightly in gauze. Bound all together, they look like a mummy. She's making a cast around Washington D.C., Iraq and the Mid-East, just as one might wrap a broken arm.

I know Kuan Yin can help, filling hearts with loving-kindness. When one calls her name, she will do anything that she can to help. I believe she is real and that she can do something about the killing. I don't know how much. I'm in such a mood. I want her to fix everything. Now I see her. She's underneath the countries, holding up that part of the map."

"I'm showing you how light it really is," explains Kuan Yin.

"Kuan Yin wants to alleviate all pain, suffering and hunger on the earth," comments Lena. "I'm going to be quite for a moment as I'm now going somewhere with Kuan Yin and I'm not sure where it is."

"I don't mind waiting," I comment.

"I get the impression that she takes the war drama kind of lightly. When I ask her to do something about it, she tells me she knows the whole story and it's already over."

"You're at page ten but I understand the entire evolution. In reality, it's already over. It's a dream. Remember? You're living a dream. It's very complicated to hold the dream and live the dream. You are learning the art of juggling the dream and the world of dreams. Nobody really gets hurt.

Sometimes parents don't want their children to watch certain cartoons. However, there's an important message one can glean from these episodes. For example, Wile E. Coyote can get blown up. After that, he may get squished by a bunch of rocks. Over and over he can defy destruction. How many times are you going to feel sorry for him when he keeps coming back?" Kuan Yin inquires.

"I don't know how to be in this world. It upsets me," laments Lena. "Kuan Yin has disappeared for a moment. I'm seeing a sweeping landscape of beautiful mountains and cliffs. I see Kuan Yin and Buddha carved deeply in the rocks. Now, Kuan Yin is showing me a beautiful canyon."

"Even the earth is reflective of the different kinds of evolution," intervenes Kuan Yin. "There is the hellish aspect, deserts and other unlivable places. There are places on the earth where people get hurt. However, there are also places of incredible peace and beauty. All of these Evolutionary Potentials are being played out at the same time, somewhere on the earth. You can come to that place of peace."

"I'm afraid I'll forget the others who are suffering," frets Lena.

"This is the very reason the saints don't immediately enter Nirvana. Even after they've attained perfect enlightenment, they cannot abide the thought of even one soul suffering. That is why *you*, Lena, are still here. Our session is complete, for now," concludes Kuan Yin.

"Kuan Yin is showing me a special place in the canyon," comments Lena. "She is leaving us a gift, Hope. She has made a circle with white rocks and at the center; she has placed some vases with flowers in them. She's shape shifting, telling me it's time for her to leave. She's a willow branch. Buddha. Oh now she's a chubby Kuan Yin floating in a bubble."

"Hope, paint me as a big fat Kuan Yin. Tsk! Tsk! I'm not at all pleased with the thin body type standards of your culture," Kuan Yin scolds as she disappears, floating down the stream and into the universe.

After being counted back up, Lena explained what she had witnessed during her trance:

"Everything was moving so quickly at one point that I couldn't find the words for what I was seeing. During the passage where we were flying over the carved faces in the cliffs, I knew we were somewhere in South Asia. Then, I saw a procession of monks dressed in red robes. They were walking along the cliffs and chanting. At that very moment, Kuan Yin giggled and said to me, 'See what I can get men to do for me? If this is what they need to do to feel closer to me or to their idea of God, then let them!'

There was another time during our discussion when I was in so much pain. I think it was just when Kuan Yin was explaining how life circumstances are either karmic or voluntary. At that very moment she was explaining how she already "knows the end of the world": how the "drama is already over". Somehow, I knew she wasn't being irreverent or flip about the war. She just knows. And during that moment, in a flash, the pain I'd been experiencing was gone. I was reading in the *Lotus Sutra* that the reason for all Kuan Yin's heads and arms is she is demonstrating how she can take on the images of a vast variety of people."

Commentary: Evolutionary Potentials and Personal Resonance: the Power of Free Will

We create everything from our thoughts. As ruler and protector of waking reality, what ego wants, ego usually gets. Depending upon the focus and clarity of its originator, however, the end result of a particular vision may or may not manifest exactly as intended. There are no boundaries on what one can attract in life. Because an inexperienced or disorganized attractor has the potential to manifest a hodgepodge life, it's essential to clearly delineate categories for manifestation.

Like tending specific areas of a garden, then, each category must be provided with the necessary components for success. One may choose from and/or modify the following example manifestation categories: a happy family, good health, fulfilling career, social responsibility, etc. Each requires its own unique nurturing and care. Each represents a simultaneous category or *channel* for one's personal Evolutionary Potentials. One can then insert, mix and match or entirely delete projected beliefs and intentions.

Waking reality will display all the 3-D sense data mirroring the predominant beliefs and emotions of your 'presenting' Evolutionary Potential. This may be a distinctly wide or narrow wave energy membrane containing magnetized reality-parameters extending within and beyond the physical boundaries of one's flesh: what could be considered one's *aura*. Depending upon its tonal amplitude, it will, in turn, attract expansive or limiting reality-parameters from the undulating and layered gestalt of all Evolutionary Potentials. The wider the band: the more inclusive. In personal relationships, these bands will either intertwine or veer away from one another.

Reality is actually the exact opposite of what is assumed. Time and space do not offer a window where human consciousness is played out. Instead, powerful convergences of beliefs and emotions create the aforementioned karmic *windows of opportunity* within the time/space continuum. Reality-parameters will gravitate in through those windows. Understanding how to 'plug in' desirable belief and emotion variables into both in and out of time thought streams is key.

Hence, it is our responsibility, Kuan Yin instructs, to "imagine the possibilities of something greater than is right here": pleasing and expansive Evolutionary Potentials. One's thought/resonance layers and the beliefs attracting them could be compared to certain geographical configurations attracting and repelling particular weather patterns. The resonance of love and acceptance will likely, therefore, contrast dramatically with the resonance of blame and anger.

Your personal vibration defines and determines your *attraction potential* of all reality-parameters needed to complete a movie (i.e. ego's waking reality). Just acknowledging the availability of this innate skill can initiate the process of magnetizing more expansive Evolutionary Potentials for replacing any self-imposed barriers to success.

14
Dragon Riding Kuan Yin

June 27, 2004: "Humanity has created itself around the 'survival of the fittest' belief and the fearful belief that there is 'not enough'. Unfortunately, many individuals really believe there are not enough resources for everyone...Any war and any other dilemma focusing on hate, fear and murder is based on the belief of not enough and the illusion of survival of the fittest."
-*Kuan Yin*

The countdown having gone smoothly, Lena arrives first at her safe place and then her sacred place. Once again seeing the fishing village and giant statue of Kuan Yin, (that she previously perceived), Lena wonders why she is so attracted to and seemingly familiar with this particular locale: a place she believes to be somewhere in Japan or southeast China. Recently she again found (while searching the Internet), what she believed was a very similar location; a fishing village having a giant statue of Kuan Yin watching compassionately from the mountaintop.

"Sometimes I wonder why the men of the village ever allowed such a giant statue of her to be erected," reflects Lena. "She stands through all kinds of weather: rain, sun and even earthquakes. Giant but peaceful!

Kuan Yin is revealing to me this steadfast symbol of herself. I'm so drawn to this particular statue. I don't know why. I want to ask Kuan Yin how to forgive those who abuse power. How can I stay detached? Forgive? I'm going to be silent for a moment so that she can respond or lead me to another subject.

Kuan Yin is changing back to her pastime of riding a dragon on the ocean. In her right hand, she holds a globe. In her left hand she carries a staff. I'm not sure what the globe represents. Now I'm here with her. She is beautiful, maybe around forty-five years old. She is sitting in her traditional position. I notice how the folds of her robe seem to be much more than cloth. They seem to hold a mysterious energy. Now, she is pouring us some tea, Hope. Seated upon a beautiful piece of cloth, together, we're near a beautiful waterfall."

"Just be with me, now," entices Kuan Yin. "We can sip tea and be together."

"This is really nice," agrees Lena. "What's wonderful about this whole experience is that Kuan Yin is completely present. She's not just here with me. She's *in* my heart quadrant. She's *in* me. She has an astonishing ability to be present.

I'm seeing how one's mind can distract, can come between one another. Here and now (with Kuan Yin), there is no space between our complete focused attentions. The energy is unbroken, continuous. It's like a meditation.

Even as she is pouring tea, I feel a thread, a connection—the real possibility that she can be carried within us, *me*. I'm going to drink the tea in honor of her presence.

Kuan Yin, then, invites me to partake, saying: "You, Hope, can drink it too."

"She's going to take me on a journey. I look into the cup of tea and am suddenly going into the universe. I'm trailing on her robes. However, they're not really robes. There is something important about her clothing, her flowing garments. She can use them to demonstrate, to create like a canvas."

"I knew Hope would understand that," Kuan Yin then exclaims. "The folds of the material can become any reality, for example, landscapes, other universes."

"We are flying in the universe," continues Lena. "However, at the same time we seem to be flying over America. Miles and miles of farmland! This time, instead of taking me to Iraq, Kuan Yin is taking me to what appears to be the state of Texas.

Today, we are focusing on petroleum and what it represents," interprets Lena: "money and power! Kuan Yin seems to be telling me that the energy of certain oil families (including the parents and grandparents) can also include anyone in or out of body attracted to them. There is an intense need for money. I can feel it. It is almost as if they're suffocating and the oil helps them to breathe," comments Lena. "There are the [aforementioned] families as well as their ancestral legacies to oil."

"They need the oil because it is like oxygen for them," reveals Kuan Yin. "There are some beings that need particular elements. You know how a physician may prescribe specific vitamins or minerals for a patient? The Vedas often recommend certain stones, gems or crystals be carried for one's protection or general well being.

For some reason, some energies require the element of oil to breathe, (whether metaphorical or not). And, of course, breath is *life*. Certain individuals need these elements. Over time, misguided forces; disembodied *spirit energies* (souls) hovering over the earth, have created these particular families.

Everyone creates (expansive or limiting) realities based on their own personal beliefs. However, some beliefs are so powerful as to potentially create limiting realities over and over. There is now so much global investment in the belief that oil is life. The energy has been built up to such an extent as to attract similar out-of-body spirits. Someone who is actually quite weak can appear strong when 'backed' by these.

Indeed, behind the above families is a powerful mass of souls who believe strongly that oil is life. They also have the mindset that it is the only thing keeping them in existence. In other words, if the belief goes, so do they.

So, this inaccurate belief system, this 'untruth' has magnified itself. And as in all inaccurate belief systems, nature will oppose it because it is too dense," decrees Kuan Yin. "Conversely, Nirvana is very light, very ethereal. Untruth must be broken down into no thought. This untruth will come up against a great opposition."

Continuing to describe the disk, Lena states: "It is very hard in texture. Kuan Yin is lifting it up like a mountain. It's like a giant disk of great density. She's balancing it on her staff while continuing to ride upon the dragon across the ocean. Nevertheless, she still maintains a sense of hope.

I ask her how she will dissolve this hard mass constructed of the limiting belief systems. She tells me the energy of 'good' will reach the souls like a prayer. Kuan Yin is also telling me the disk cannot just be destroyed. If that strategy is ever attempted, many will perish. I'm confused," confesses Lena. "Certainly, I don't want anyone to die. What's to be done with it; this strange and dense energy?"

"What do you think we can do with it?" Kuan Yin casts this crucial question back to Lena.

Just then, my pen ran dry. Why was this happening at such a critical time? Was it destiny? Not having the luxury to continue my pondering, I knew more pens were in the cabinet at the other end of the living room. Leaping up, I say somewhat awkwardly, "Wait just a moment, Lena. I'm out of ink. I just need to go get another pen."

"I just understood it!" exclaims Lena. "Just when you jumped up to get another pen, I finally understood what Kuan Yin is trying to tell me. Kuan Yin says everything being spoken and written about the Iraq War is shedding light on this limiting belief system, slowly dissolving the disk.

Each of us will help to break it down slowly. And people will evolve to understand it," concludes Lena, with a sigh of relief.

"Many people are unaware they buy into this belief system," notes Kuan Yin. "Nevertheless, they go on believing the only way they'll survive is to have money. The [above-discussed] oil families represent the majority's relationship with prosperity and survival. Humanity has *created itself* around the 'survival of the fittest' belief and the fearful belief that there are not enough resources.

Unfortunately, many individuals really believe there are not enough resources for everyone. Additionally, the disembodied souls are not aware they don't really need oil to breathe; that they are fabricating situations they believe they need to survive. So many have made an 'agreement', then, that there isn't enough. Any war and any other dilemma focusing on hate, fear and murder is based on the belief of not enough and the illusion of survival of the fittest."

"I'm feeling as though I'm underwater and unable to breathe," says Lena.

"It took a long time for your planet to evolve into this crisis," continues Kuan Yin. "We are witnessing the greed and bad behavior of certain individuals. It is a very potent time. People are learning. And what they learn also sets them [the above-mentioned individuals] free. They will no longer be trapped in their own belief system. People will begin to get sparks of light. There will increasingly be more and more sparks which will erode the darkness of confusion," Kuan Yin prophesizes.

[Here, Kuan Yin asserts that certain members of the above families can be very "weak energies". According to the Goddess, in such circumstances, more powerful (out-of-body) energies "can therefore go through them; using the earth bodies for their own purposes".]

Isn't it curious Lena? Think about what drives you in your life and how many of those beliefs are not serving you well. I'm very grateful for our connection, for this opportunity to meet with you."

"Kuan Yin is touching the arm—no the *shoulder* of this belief system. She is putting her hand on the 'shoulder' with utmost compassion," describes Lena.

"I'm sorry for your anguish," consoles Kuan Yin, gently.

"I understand now," Lena exclaims softly. "Many of these energies are not in human form. Kuan Yin is putting her hand on the thoughts that make up the dense disk. Now I truly see what she is doing. It's alchemy."

"Yes. There's a balance that makes something holistic and in truth." responds Kuan Yin. "What I am placing my hand upon is a dense conglomeration of stuck energy made up of certain ideas. Naturally, not all ideas are included in this energy. It needs certain elements, things sprinkled into it gradually.

Having compassion for the 'untruth', that is what's missing. I'm sending compassion into this rock. One needs to slowly add elements of insight to reach truth. It's a good time to ask ourselves to look at any lies we are telling ourselves. It's a powerful time to examine one's own thoughts and the thoughts of the people of the world.

Let us all reflect upon the *great mix* of free will and karma. Reread the past chapters and ponder what I have said. Karma is intricate, detailed. One cannot dwell on only one particle of this great collective energy. Your life is but one frame of an entire reel of film," instructs Kuan Yin, reiterating concepts from previous sessions.

Everyone has her or his part. Some don't perform any of their part as they have incomplete or incorrect belief systems. Sometimes it seems as if this world is completely chaotic and sometimes it really is. However, there is a corrective force, an actual physical force."

"Kuan Yin is showing me this force," says Lena, describing what she is witnessing: "It's a pendulum. No. It's more like a spiral. It seems very complicated. I want to understand, to know more about this structure…"

"You don't need to necessarily understand everything about the forces—the dynamics of the universe. However, you need to have faith that the process is guided and correct, that it is ultimately good and that there exists a kind of cosmic steering of evolution, a reason for all of this," counsels Kuan Yin. "It's already finished! The past, present and future have already occurred.

Events that seem so cruel and unforgivable…Have faith and trust that even these happenings are ultimately an expression of goodness. Certain religions say things are planned; everything is already worked out. In a very real sense, this is so. All the pain and suffering! It's like a dream. It doesn't go on forever. The suffering does end."

"I want to ask Kuan Yin something," Lena begins.

"Lena, you need to develop your faith and your trust," interrupts Kuan Yin. "Please try to work on that. Look into your childhood. You came into the world surrounded by violence. Thus, you developed a belief system around fear. Try to remember the universe is on the right course. You no longer have to live life through a veil of fear. You can go beyond it to a place of peace and trust.

Now it is time to end the session, for today. It's difficult to let you go. These times together are a way for me to give and communicate my loving compassion. I love when people realize and validate the gifts I send. I'll always be there to comfort and help those in need. I delight in helping others."

"I realize that the tea party is ending," comments Lena. "I touch her hand and say goodbye. I've never known anyone to love me as much as she does. She is still riding the dragon. She is holding the globe and the staff with the dense disk on top of it as she rides away."

Commentary: Collective Agreements, Invested Identities and Kuan Yin's Law of Compassion

Like currents in the ocean propelling movement of an iceberg, fluctuating brainwaves form the underlying mechanical scaffolding for human consciousness. Having a 360-degree vantage point, ego-centered consciousness, with practice; has the potential to evaluate content within the slower alpha, theta and delta mind bandwidths as well as the faster gamma mind bandwidth.

Ego's predilection, however, is to focus on waking reality. This preference can (when skillfully utilized) create the perfect arena for attracting our most desired reality through daily affirmation and visualization.

Kuan Yin states that it is one's experience of the earth plane that could offer spiritual completion. Here, the soul can finally resolve any self-constructed 'wells' of limiting beliefs.

However, there appears to be a polarizing relationship between the "not enough" and "better than" mindsets as well as "survival of the fittest". These beliefs can potentially volley a soul between feelings of inadequacy, superiority and competition; possibly for lifetimes. According to Kuan Yin, the above limiting beliefs have now condensed into a dense disk: a menacing energy juggernaut potentially responsible for myriad, entrapping realities.

As discussed, there are Mass as well as Personal Evolutionary Potentials. One could regard our present global Mass EP (or paradigm) as just one of infinite parallel energy spheres. Each will be dominated by their peculiar belief sets and vibration. While every other parallel EP remains physically out of reach of waking reality, earth is the operative focal point.

Thoughts and emotions springing from various political and other unifying issues are registered as a mass *Point (s) of Intention*. This magnetic force ultimately draws one or more Mass EP's, determining the direction of a community, nation or even the entire world.

Historically, certain leaders have exploited this by generating beneficial or unbeneficial points of intention. Any Mass EP event can affect, to the degree of participation, those who've contributed to the original thought form.

Providing specific visualizations and meditations, Kuan Yin demonstrates how *focused intent* can assist and accelerate the attraction of beneficial Personal as well as Mass EPs.

15
Touching the Tree

July 2, 2004: "You were exposed to your traumatic childhood to learn about compassion. A place of extreme sensitivity was *carved out in your soul*. However, you mistook the meaning of your childhood. You believed you were destined to be a victim when in fact the trauma opened you to compassion. You can help teach the world about empathy. If you'd rather use the words, 'loving kindness' that's fine. Empathy or loving-kindness! They are the same. But remember, they're very different from guilt or pity. Having true empathy is to understand another's pain and suffering from a place of power. Your job is to also create new possibilities."
-*Kuan Yin*

Arriving at her "sacred place", Lena immediately begins to speak:
"Kuan Yin has a sense of humor going on today. She's coming to me like a good friend one gets to know over a period of time; a very good friend who will never abandon you. This sensation of love I have right now seems familiar and yet I don't believe I've ever experienced it on earth.

She's sitting on a flower. Maybe it's a lotus. I'm not sure. It's interesting how as you were counting me down, Hope, I was there on the flower with Kuan Yin. It had a huge stem and with every number of the countdown, the stem grew a little more. It was like Jack in the Beanstalk. I'm not certain of the significance of that," Lena reflects.

"There is a wiry texture covering the stem. We, Kuan Yin and I, are teetering on the top of this flower or tree and looking down. I don't know whether this symbolizes anything. We're both lighthearted. Maybe the flower in the sky is reflective of my mood. I'm on vacation in my *real* life. My work is behind me, for now. I think both Kuan Yin and I are more relaxed and playful.

Kuan Yin looks very traditional. Her hands are folded together. The thick cloth of her costume is folded perfectly. Just as in the previous session, I'm reminded of the significance of the folds. I'm having an interesting vision that I haven't thought about in many years. I see a beautiful tree where I used to go when I was a teenager. It stands majestic, atop the rolling hills behind the house where I grew up.

When I was lonely and sad about my life, I used to go there. I had my black light and my Moody Blues tape and I would go sit near the tree to listen to my music. Kuan Yin is at the tree looking very luminous. I see the bark of the tree, which looks very real, very three-dimensional. For some reason, Kuan Yin is touching the trunk of the tree.

She suddenly seems very small next to me and she wants me to touch the tree. I'm not sure why. There is a tiny bird, with pretty feathers in its nest. It is about the size of a wren. I see the texture of the tree. I think it might be a birch. I'm not sure. 'Why should I touch the tree,' I ask. She's telling me that I created the tree, that it is another realm I was able to visit because life was too painful and lonely at home."

"You created the tree. You create your whole world with thoughts," assures Kuan Yin.

"Every time I try to touch the tree, Kuan Yin wants to help me touch it. There's something different about this conversation. Usually we work on something about the earth. Because we're revisiting my childhood, I get the impression Kuan Yin's trying to show me something that maybe I created in my childhood."

"Well, do we all create our reality?" Kuan Yin asks of Lena.

"I think she's going to answer her own question," comments Lena, from her trance.

"Yes, you can create your reality. Once you free yourself from the negative effects of karma. I know it is sometimes difficult to differentiate between free will and karma. Focus upon your free will and your ability to create reality. I'm optimistic and hopeful you can do this."

"Now, I'm feeling really hopeful, too. I'm still there at the tree. The little bird now has babies. It's not scared; it's not leaving. Kuan Yin is lifting the bird and appreciating it."

"Appreciate and marvel at everything. Especially nature! Learn from nature. Learn the way it works so you can know how to be in the world."

"We're looking around this place," remarks Lena. "It is pretty neat. It has a cornfield like the one behind the house where I grew up. I'm looking towards the cornfield from the tree that I created. It's a different perspective. I don't believe I ever looked in that direction before.

Sounds like I can visualize anything I want," Lena concedes.

"How counterproductive—chastising children for daydreaming," Kuan Yin laments. Focus. Certain masters want you to learn to do this."

"But what's the point?" Lena inquires. I've read some New Age theories, about creating reality; the importance of one's mindset, etc."

"The point is not to drag the negative past or future into the present. Understanding the possibilities of the present! It's a skill useful for discovering the divine."

"Kuan Yin is showing me something; a tube, I think. I don't fully understand this diagram. It is as if one end is the past, the other the future. The middle of the tube, the present, is our way, our *vehicle* for changing reality."

"You slip into the universe, while living in this dream, this present. Your escape hatch is *right here.*"

"I'm not drawn to doing this, however I need to understand more," contemplates Lena. "It is apparently like meditating upon a beautiful place, I suppose. The more one dwells on the vision of the beautiful place, the more real it becomes.

I'm realizing I *can* touch the tree, that it really still is here after all these years. Kuan Yin is going to direct me to more books on the subject of creating reality, how to create new possibilities for myself. She says I shouldn't limit myself with ideas from childhood."

"Thoughts can influence the way the world can go," continues Kuan Yin. "What a radical concept! Everyone having loving kindness! With practice, a reality is created somewhere having that very consciousness of loving kindness. Such practice also draws one to those loving kindness planes of consciousness."

"During the week, I was getting insights, quick visions of how my children would be when they're grown. I heard Michael, my son, saying something in the future in a deep and manly voice. I also saw Marina, my daughter, as a teenager. She was dancing and having such a good time. I was thinking how it is so important to be present when interacting with children. How they help keep us in the present.

They grow up so fast. All week long I was also marveling how wonderful it is to have a family. Kuan Yin just loves children. She tells me how they're much more our teachers then we sometimes realize. And that many adults do not value the children as our teachers."

"Yes. If you were just to look to the children as examples for living you're life, you can know what to do," affirms Kuan Yin.

"I wonder if that means I should choose a vocation having to do more with children?" ponders Lena. "They certainly require that one be present."

"Everything we learn from them we can apply to the world," continues Kuan Yin addressing Lena's concerns. "It would be wonderful if all of society could do this, could approach and resolve issues in such a 'childlike' and innocent way."

"Kuan Yin is suddenly showing me a globe. She's showing me what appears to be a cloud of stagnant male energy: globs of heavy, thick and stale yang energy. I don't know how we are going to get through this."

"Earth is a place to live out karma," expounds Kuan Yin. "There are other places, other possibilities. Don't get too dragged down where the karma is thick. Concentrate on creating the possibilities."

"Kuan Yin is saying this because I came from extreme trauma I believed it was my lot in life to be…I'm not sure what Kuan Yin is saying here. Oh now I understand. I believed I was meant to suffer, to be a victim."

"You were exposed to your (traumatic) childhood to learn about and understand compassion. A place of extreme sensitivity was carved out in your soul. However, you mistook the meaning of your childhood. You believed you were destined to be a victim when in fact the trauma opened you to compassion.

You can help teach the world about empathy. If you'd rather use the words 'loving kindness', that's fine. Empathy or loving-kindness! They're the same. But remember, they're very different from guilt or pity. Having true empathy is to understand other's pain and suffering from a place of power. Your job is to also create new possibilities."

"We're back at the tree. I'm touching the bark. Kuan Yin is telling me the tree is as real as my life is."

"You can practice by coming here (to this place of peace and harmony in your mind) and envision various things happening."

"It sounds like there is a lot of power in doing that. Kuan Yin is showing me a little place up in the corner of the room. I'm looking through a telescope at myself," Lena's voice trails off.

"Remember that this place, the corn field where you grew up, is just as real as you laying on the bed right here and now. We'll leave a couple of cows in the field."

"OK. Now I'm helping Kuan Yin leave some cows in the field. They're so real. I'm going to try and remember this process in everything I do," Lena concludes, apparently quite near to waking consciousness.

"Are you ready to come back?" I inquire.

"Yes. I think I just have to be counted up a little bit. Oh, I'm at the number two, so just count me up from there."

When Lena returned from alpha to beta state, she once again remarked upon how Kuan Yin came to her as increasingly more three-dimensional and vibrant. According to Lena's description, Kuan Yin had manifested as "more real and human-like" than during any of their previous encounters.

Commentary: Visualizing Anything

So often, people wonder about their purpose here on earth. Some do not believe they can make a difference; that as individuals they are powerless. Others believe that attaining great wealth and position is the ultimate goal. Yet, throughout the sessions, Kuan Yin has been clear that only through understanding and experiencing the full spectrum of one's humanity can one make a difference. This does not require great wealth or position. Nor does it require an ascetic lifestyle. Preferable to a monastic or otherwise carefully formulated life, it is the ups and downs of one's life, fostering one's spiritual transcendence.

One method for achieving this kind of mastery of the ego utilizes the imagination and creative force and is termed *Beneficial Emulation*. Fads and fashion crazes are examples of how natural emulation occurs all the time. One's unique and enlightened interpretation, indeed *expression* of a desirable trait or quality (benefiting both you as well as others) is the definition of *Beneficial Emulation*. Being aware of the potent combinations of all your seven innate forces, you could perfect the art of attracting the most beneficial reality-parameters *for you*. Because of the qualities She embodies, perhaps the highest mastery of this skill is emulating Kuan Yin's infinite forms.

Parting the *darkness*, visualizing the possibilities for a better world is, as Kuan Yin states, a skill that can be developed and practiced while here on earth. Developing love and compassion while experiencing life's challenges, according to Kuan Yin, leads to true divinity. She demonstrates how one can hone his/her spiritual abilities while living a "realistic life".

Examples of how visions create unique and indelible residues, Kuan Yin's metamorphisms spontaneously billow forth as evolutions from the original thought or emotional imprint. Her shape shifting reminds us of our own divinity, our greatest potential to visualize limitless love and forgiveness.

Insisting that each such arrangement, each probable reality, is similar to a still frame in a reel of a motion picture, Kuan Yin explains that any one point in one's life (or still frame) represents levels of infinitude. Like the tree Lena experienced from her childhood still miraculously existing outside of time and space, each still frame created has durability, the potential to live on eternally.

16
The Divinity of Humanity

July 9, 2004: "Do not believe that your humanity prevents you from being spiritual. Know that this earth drama doesn't mean spirituality does not exist on the earth plane. Try to be forgiving and objective when enduring your own earthly drama. Indeed, one's approach to one's own life drama can actually affect the outcome. That is, certain interactive strategies can render an ordinary drama, spiritual."
-*Kuan Yin*

On this, the eve of Lena's surgery, she spoke of her family members and their differing reactions to the surgery and any uncertain outcome. Even though the prognosis was good, Lena noticed how each family member had his or her own way of processing fear.

Lena had also been reading instructions about making a Will, attempting to be more proactive and attentive to information on the subject provided in books, videos and, very recently, even in her dreams. Worrying about the success of her upcoming surgery, she noticed the children seemed nervous, and somewhat irritable. Additionally, her husband seemed overly busy, unwilling to deal with any fear or apprehension concerning the outcome.

Lena went on to mention that (in the book she was presently reading), the author had focused upon various sightings and communications with Kuan Yin (in primarily Asian countries). In one chapter, he mentioned a particular peasant woman, noting that she, out of all the people in her village, was the one who could most profoundly invoke Kuan Yin.

At the same time, Lena also very much looked forward to healing the debilitating pain that originated in her shoulder, radiating down through her entire left arm. Now calm, prepared for her transpersonal countdown, Lena snuggled into her warm comforter. Upon reaching full trance state, Lena immediately recognized Kuan Yin:

"I see the folds of her garment, again, so thick and intricate. Kuan Yin is here observing a lotus. However, she's more than observing it; she's *being* with it, meditating upon it, *appreciating* it. She's focused very intently on the lotus as if she is conversing with it. It's an interesting thing to see Kuan Yin relating to a flower so intently. Now, the lotus is floating away. Kuan Yin is encouraging me to talk to her."

"Ask me a question," coaxes Kuan Yin.

"I guess what I want to ask is how best to worship her, get on the path that ultimately leads to peace, Nirvana. What is also occurring for me, today, is that I want to ask her about the colonies of monks and male-dominated religions.

There's a lot going on in my life: family obligations, job, school and now this surgery. There appear to be many different ways to worship Kuan Yin and yet one can still get quite discouraged. I'm going to take a moment to listen, to see what Kuan Yin wants to tell me about that."

"OK. I'll be writing all of this down," I assure Lena.

"Oh, I'm hearing Kuan Yin telling me something."

"You're too distracted by those issues. Put them aside and really look at the flower with me."

"I'm looking at the flower and watching how Kuan Yin relates to it," continues Lena. "I'm seeing how the act of relating to a flower appears to be so simple. Yet, it takes a tremendous amount of courage to make such a simple act important.

I understand now how busyness can be a real distraction, how it can create 'made up' realities. Being present means an absence of past and future. I'm seeing how bringing the mind into the present is the link to eternity and that true meditation is the acceptance of no past or future. I realize these are amazingly brave concepts, that there are only moments upon moments to be lived. It's almost inconceivable.

Usually Kuan Yin takes me on a journey somewhere. Or there is an elaborate backdrop. Today, however, we are in 'no place'. Against only a backdrop of air, Kuan Yin sits; intent upon really being with a flower. It's so interesting. There is a tremendous difference between that consciousness of really being with something and, for instance, living a life. It's as if the life is the *dream*!"

"The best you can do," continues Kuan Yin "is to live a life of integrity and authenticity. Do the best you can and be honest with yourself and others. There is a collective agreement that this life you live here on earth is the only reality. Therefore, you just have to play along."

"How does one live on both of these planes [of reality] and make it work?"

"Do not believe that your humanity prevents you from being spiritual. Know that this earth drama doesn't mean spirituality doesn't exist on the earth plane. Try to be forgiving and objective when enduring your own earthly drama. Indeed, one's approach to one's own life drama can actually affect the greater outcome. That is, certain interactive strategies can render an ordinary drama, spiritual. Don't fall into the trap of ego and money. Don't be too concerned whether the drama you're experiencing is a result of karma. Rather, emphasize the concept that we are all one, that no one is better than the other. You are all sacred energies and everyone is as sacred as the next."

"I do not quite understand all of what Kuan Yin is saying. I've heard they can make gold from base metal. Oh. I think I'm starting to comprehend. Kuan Yin is talking about *alchemy*."

"Yes. When one brings spirit into the human realm, it can even *spiritualize* matter. Matter can then become lighter, (indeed *liberated*), not so dense, as before."

"Kuan Yin tells me we are all spiritual beings who have taken birth here. She says the earth plane is a wonderful opportunity to develop humility and compassion. She's also telling me there is something to the whole philosophy behind meditation. But, there are tons of different rituals. Which ones are better, I wonder?"

"Those souls who've chosen that path are trying to bring spirit into matter. Instead of pushing paper all day, they perform rituals and ceremonies. However, the peasant woman who works at home is no less important, spiritual than the monks. Anyone can bring spirit into his or her daily life. Being a monk is just one choice. Don't get discouraged that you're not a monk."

"Maybe I'll find or purchase a special flower. I was going to ask Kuan Yin to help guide the surgeon and to help the babies and cancer patients who are in the hospital where I'll be having my surgery."

"What a wonderful place to be, to bring me *alive*!"

"Kuan Yin is very excited about being asked to be with and talk to me during my hospital stay. Because she'll be there with me, she can also go and help those who request her presence. She is emphasizing that she can only come to those who *ask* for her help. She's telling me to do the exercises, to meditate upon a flower and to ask for her energy to be present with me during my stay at the hospital. She tells me there will be more realizations to come while I'm in the hospital and in future communications."

Commentary: Rendering an Ordinary Drama, Spiritual: The Power of the Word

One of the primary reasons for Kuan Yin's coming to earth is to remind us of the power of the spoken word: that individual words have their uniquely-structured "tonal wave mass" undulating and attracting or repelling specific reality-parameters.

Any spoken sequence of words might be thought of as a kind of "tonal wave mass *score*", having unique dynamic properties. Indeed, each impulse has its own distinct signature and nuance: a customized energy born of one's personal beliefs and intentions. Beneficial or unbeneficial emotions will help to determine the overall resonance. It is the continuous coalescing of one's (karmic and instinctual) wave impulses with one's word choice that constitutes a weak or powerful energy *field*.

Like major or minor key concertos, wave impulses combined with certain words can have an uplifting or subduing mood effect. Kuan Yin's famous *om mani padi* mantra exemplifies how wave impulses combined with key word sets can work at an *energetic* level.

Now, Kuan Yin's term 'tonal wave-mass' may seem, to some, a paradoxical way to define the physical properties of a word. Yet, sound waves must interact with some existing mass form to be propagated forward.

There is an interesting story that goes along with this. One evening, I had been writing about sound, affirmations and the power of the word. In particular, I was trying to elucidate how each affirmation produces a unique 'tonal wave'. Falling asleep shortly thereafter, I heard Kuan Yin in a dream, quite loudly, correct me: "'Tonal wave' affirmations" isn't quite correct, she explained. "The proper phrase is tonal wave-*mass* affirmations! Each word's emitted sound wave vibrationally energizes the mass it interacts with!"

Hopefully, you now understand the relationship between sound wave dynamics and how affirmations work. The mass (or medium) is, of course, individual air or water particles. Because of the vibrational interaction with the air or water molecules, any one word has a specific attraction potential. It should be noted that sound attraction processes differ from light and gravity physics.

The relative wavelength of a word will attract or repel actual energy units according to its connotative and/or denotative vibrational 'weight'.

This is a crucial piece to Kuan Yin's "wave and wind" metaphor. Acting as the *wind*, free will carries one's strongly or weakly resonating karmic *wave*.

Even in the womb words and their accompanying tone's create a profound bond between mother and child. The fetus' heartbeat and metabolism and other cellular balances are believed to be affected by, for example, the mother's particularly happy or sad words and tonalities. The relationship between mother and fetus, therefore, is presumed to be so profound that the fetus also does not distinguish its own tonalities and rhythms from those of its mother. It is these primal tonalities between mother and babe that 'set the stage' for birth and beyond.

This dynamic is the basis for various theories concerning the relationship between positive affirmations and tonal cellular manipulation. Similar to fetuses identifying with the mother's tonal stimuli, adult cells can follow the directives of certain words and tonalities. Harmonious words and tonalities, therefore, may help to balance cellular and Soul (Core) Essence ebb and flow whereas dissonant words and tonalities could create discord and imbalance.

If you do not approve of the reality-parameters currently defining your life, it is probably time to rethink your entire word repertoire. To do this effectively, though, you will need to take an uncompromising look at your beliefs. The greatest encumbrances to one's natural flow are guilt-generating thoughts and their corresponding words dwelling in the conscious and unconscious minds.

17
The Divine Realms

July 29, 2004: "Parents are god-like in their power over children. Your parent's lives were also lived in fear. However, there are realms where there is absolutely no fear. In such (divine) realms, realization is complete. Fear is completely absent from these realms. On this earth where people feel so separate there does not exist a feeling of oneness."

-*Kuan Yin*

Having spoken with Lena on several occasions since her surgery, I knew the procedure performed on her shoulder, though more complicated than originally expected, had been quite successful. Well into the recovery phase, Lena mentioned she was meeting with a physical therapist a few times a week. When we met again today for hypnosis, it was approximately three weeks following the time of her surgery.

Saying that she had been having intense dreams and repeatedly waking up at about four in the morning, Lena mentioned she'd like to experiment tape-recording herself during a self-induced trance. Wondering out loud whether, after being absent from hypnosis for a while, she would be able to achieve a satisfactory trance level; Lena signaled she was ready to be counted down. Reaching her 'safe place' and then her 'sacred place', Lena immediately began to speak:

"Yes, I'm here in my usual bamboo grove. I see the waterfall and the rocks. I see a Koi pond, colorful fish swimming in a pool of water. Kuan Yin is here. She is neither young nor old. She's curious, inquisitive, acknowledging it has been awhile since we've conversed together. She says she heard my prayers while I was in the hospital.

I wanted to go to the different hospital wards to bring Kuan Yin's energy and my own compassion and caring into the rooms where the children and adult patients were recovering. But I was too weak. I was experiencing too much pain.

All I could do was to pray for the woman lying in the bed beside mine. She was very sick. I prayed for the image of Kuan Yin to come to her, to comfort her. Each time I tried to envision Kuan Yin; however, I saw the image of Guadalupe, instead. I don't know why. Maybe, that was the image the woman could understand, relate to best.

Kuan Yin is asking me to sit by her. We're just looking around at the surroundings: the Mosques, bamboo, the Koi Pond. She's telling me my issues around fear still need to be resolved. Her words are making me remember how fearful my brothers and I were of being left alone with my father, how I grew up to see the world through a *filter of fear.*"

"Parents are god-like in their power over children. Your parent's lives were also lived in fear," begins Kuan Yin. "However, there are realms where there is absolutely no fear. In such divine realms, realization is complete. Fear is completely absent from these realms. On this earth where people feel so separate, there does not exist a feeling of oneness.

Notice how you comfort your children. You use stories, humor," recounts Kuan Yin, softly. "I know ultimately nothing can harm or destroy you. Fear comes from not knowing the entire truth."

"I'm being reminded by Kuan Yin of how, just last night I comforted Marina. She was crying and telling me she was afraid of monsters. I told her, 'don't cry. Monsters don't come into a house filled with love'. Kuan Yin is telling me I'm giving important coping tools to my children. Now, they will know how to comfort themselves in this sometimes-scary world. Because my parents either ignored me or told me I was ignorant, I did not get those tools.

Kuan Yin is very interested in me pursuing that issue for myself. I've done quite a bit of therapy, also breath work and other alternative practices. None of it has worked. I still don't know how to resolve my fear. Kuan Yin wants to sit with me in the beautiful garden. She's asking me to pursue my dilemma about fear."

"Yes. When you wonder about it, it is the right time to pursue that issue and change a particular way of being in the world. Find some, maybe abbreviated, way to meditate upon me each day. Take just a moment to think about me. A small ritual to keep your connection with me can be helpful. Even just acknowledging me; helps me to help you. Even a second of thought about me is very potent. If one could spend even a minute meditating instead of grand acts of devotion, it would be very powerful. No one has to commit to long, drawn-out rituals. I appreciate it, however it is not necessary."

"I'm suddenly focused upon the suffering of the world," concedes Lena.

"I too, have much sorrow about the suffering in the world," consoles Kuan Yin.

"I contribute to an international charitable group and have been sponsoring a young girl in India for over two years," explains Lena. She writes me letters and tells me how important school is, how her studies mean so much to her. However, her family is very poor. Space and resources such as food and clothing are stretched to the limit. Everyone in her family must sleep together on a single mattress. I wish I could really help. Certain places around the globe can be really scary, rough environments for people—especially young girls. There exists so much exploitation of humans."

"Just thinking kindly and giving is important. Caring about that family; even from afar, helps. Just thinking good and loving thoughts, is very potent," assures Kuan Yin.

"I want to ask Kuan Yin to help my country unite and gain more compassion. There is so much abundance here. I hope any who are afraid of sharing with others will evolve to being able to share what they have. I'm praying for more open-mindedness in our country."

"There has recently been great hope, relief among many of the citizens of the United States. There is a great anticipation of peace. Even those who've not been paying attention will be touched, affected by those who have. During hard times (difficult historical eras) people can often move towards a more spiritual mode. The past few years have been very inspiring and powerful. The 'fruits' of these challenging times will be noticed, felt. However maybe not for a few years," concludes Kuan Yin.

"Kuan Yin tells me it's time for her to go. She is giving me a present: a huge diamond. I'm asking her, 'what does it mean? What is it for?'"

"Take it with you. This is something I want to give to you for you to ponder when you meditate. When we talk again, you can tell me what you believe it means."

"OK. I'll think about what it could represent in the coming days."

"Lena, could I ask Kuan Yin something before She goes?"

"That's fine," responds Lena.

"I've wondered for some time what relationship, if any, Lena and I have shared in other lifetimes," I say.

"I'm seeing us as sisters," responds Lena, almost immediately. "I'm surprised. In that lifetime you were my younger sister. I believe we lived somewhere in China. Our hair is very dark and cut quite short."

Commentary: Choosing Love over Fear

According to Kuan Yin, earth is the most important step in our evolution. Human beliefs, intentions and desires are the driving forces from which we, as limitless beings, achieve physical manifestation and all of its complexities. The significance of the goddess's transformations is that they are metaphors explaining how to reach solutions for the challenges of modern mankind.

Actualizing a given reality involves the generation of consistent beliefs, intentions and emotions. If there is vacillation or if conflicting beliefs, intentions or emotions exist, one's magnetizing ability could be greatly compromised.

We have personal spheres of influence that are variously wide or narrow. If one is a captain of industry or celebrity, they could potentially influence millions of people. On the other hand, one who lives a somewhat secluded life probably has a rather narrow social sphere. We always have the option to develop and/or allow into consciousness, wide or narrow bands of influence.

You probably have events or people, (in your daily routine) that generate intense emotions of love or fear. For example, you're fairly confident that when meeting with beloved relatives or friends, you'll have a wonderful time. On the other hand, there might be a TV program that you've contemplated watching if only it didn't contain so much violence. The above represent two extremes of the strong, polarizing emotions of love and fear.

Everyday, the ego's powerful discriminating forces allow us to differentiate our emotions concerning the people and events in our life. Additionally, ego's distilling powers obviously facilitate pursuance of a goal or series of goals. One could not even begin implementing a goal without the ego's sublime permission and ability to focus: to be completely in the moment.

As love and fear are the primary attraction forces for any event; their vibrations, combined with *Present Positive* conscious or unconscious affirmations, can create powerful patterns expanding or contracting the 'fabric' of your present reality. Even without deliberate *Present Positive* affirming, *Points of Intention* patterns will, by default, form and reform from strong (loving) or weak (fearful) pulsations. These are the infinite probable points where simultaneous 'memories' of specific reality-parameters in the time/space curvature flow. Indeed, it is precisely because of the multidimensionality of this process that we can recall the 'future' or recreate the 'past'.

So it may be extremely pragmatic to simply notice those points during the day, when polarizing thoughts involving "better than" and "not enough" arise. Then, you could discover the unifying intention at the heart of any personal discontent.

Altering your intention allows the control, so that specific reality-parameters can then be magnetized towards you. From the earth's core, Kuan Yin's gift of the diamond represents an alternative, more balanced (personal/mass) EP paradigm. The antithesis of the "not enough" or "better than" mindsets, the diamond represents utmost compassion and spiritual abundance.

Its multifaceted properties show how when one affirms or visualizes a specific outcome, it is reverberated throughout the convergence prisms. Choosing Oneness: the stream of love connecting us all, helps to attract our most joyous and abundant realities.

18
One's Core Being
Pure Soul Essence

August 3, 2004: "Kuan Yin is showing me a Middle Eastern woman crying in her hut. I see layers and layers of, not mist, but more like different shades of thick and gooey gray lacquer. I see layers of murky stripes, smoky and jellylike. They have been clinging to this woman for hundreds of years. Underneath all of these layers is the woman's pure soul essence, the part of her that knows the processes it will take for her to be released from her karma, that which knows *everything*. This is the element of self that agrees to suffering and which knows the woman cannot be destroyed. And though this woman's reality may appear unjust, some 'unjust' bomb cannot blow her up. It cannot destroy her essence, her core being."
-Kuan Yin

It was a silent and breezeless night. Somewhere between waking and sleeping, I heard the low rustle of the medicine bells that hung on a red frayed string in my bedroom window. Tilting my head in mild surprise, I heard a whooshing sound as something quickly brushed by me. Turning on the light, I saw a small, winged animal flying in perfect circles on the ceiling. Rushing in, John flung open the window, watching incredulously as the bat flew away.

Later, calling my friend Susan, I confessed my astonishment about the whole event:

"How could a bat have come in? Having realized there was no screen, I'd opened the window only a smidgen. I may have had a momentary concern about insects getting in, but never a bat!"

Hurriedly retrieving her book on Native American medicine animals, Susan quoted a passage on the significance of encountering a bat. Borrowing the book, I later read how the bat (in such traditions) symbolizes spiritual death and rebirth. My current reality in a constant state of flux and renewal, I found the symbolism to be quite apropos.

***

Awakening the morning of the following hypnosis session after dreaming a dialogue about color and its effects on one's health and vitality, I recalled hearing a voice urge me to try on various clothes to see which color combinations were the most psychically balancing. Leaping out of bed, suspecting the dream speaker was Kuan Yin: I immediately flung open the bedroom closet. Choosing a pale pink cotton blouse and blue shorts, I was aware of an immediate change in mood, how that color combination had brightened my outlook for the day.

Anxious to go into trance and discover more about the diamond Kuan Yin had given her, Lena had mentioned that fine-tuning the wording for this particular countdown, might be of help. At Lena's request, I agreed to incorporate a specific sequence of leading and pacing verbiage. Therefore, when reaching the number eight, I recited: "and you might experience the number eight as leaning on its side, very much resembling the symbol for infinity—having no beginning and no end.

Towards the end of the countdown Lena mentioned she already had a keen sense of Kuan Yin's presence; that the Muse was close by. Entering her sacred place, Lena exclaimed how; laughing and somewhat impatient, Kuan Yin was there, waiting to greet her by the time she reached the number five. Ready to begin her discourse with Kuan Yin, Lena began:

"Every time you count me down from ten to zero," remarks Lena, "I'm fascinated when you compare the number eight with the infinity sign. Following the figure eight round and round I see how there is no beginning and no end. Then I go through it, experiencing many different and amazing realities.

This time was no different. I found myself looking through the number eight as if it were looking glasses and seeing Kuan Yin holding the huge diamond that she presented to us in the previous chapter. I'm here in my sacred place and Kuan Yin is right beside me. Placing her hand on my knee, she is like an old friend inviting me to share tea and cookies. During the countdown, however, she seemed impatient, as if she was just passing the time and having tea until I arrived. So, I'll be quiet for a moment so I can understand what she wants to tell me.

Kuan Yin is showing me something very interesting. I see the large diamond and realize it is also a flower. I see a beautiful flower and realize it is simultaneously a diamond. She is explaining how enormous wealth is not necessarily materialistic. There is the clean and clear wealth of higher consciousness. It is devoid of the depraved energy that can be attached to money. This is the 'pure wealth': the wealth of higher consciousness. I'm now being shown a dimension, a plane, where that pure wealth of consciousness is a reality. It is reality where everyone is loved, where everyone is fed and healthy. Kuan Yin is showing me around this dimension. She's showing me the good-heartedness of the energies that live here. There is someone walking on the path above, looking down to where the people are.

I'm being shown how everyone is simultaneously aware, that if someone loves, they all feel love. If someone gives, they all give. And if someone is hurting, they all feel the hurt. Those who dwell in this parallel reality are one and separate at the same time. That's why this reality works.

Because the earth plain is so dense, the dimension I've described above can't be replicated here. However, we can strive and learn from this other reality."

"You can't replicate it here on earth because not everyone would agree," Kuan Yin begins speaking.

"I'm sensing the heaviness of the earth plane now replacing the lightness there. There are many meanings to the heavy diamond. This is just one element," explains Lena.

"The [alternate] reality I'm showing you represents pure wealth. No greed is involved. Beings in this dimension desire this pure wealth because it feels good; it expands their consciousness. This is a very different approach from desiring to keep all the resources for oneself; to say that others can't have it and to also believe there is not enough," Kuan Yin discerns.

"Kuan Yin is assuring me I won't always be so worried about money. She's telling me things will get easier."

"There are a lot of people who have enormous wealth," continues Kuan Yin. "In spite of having material things they have a poverty consciousness. Wealth is a state of mind. Real wealth is not worrying about money. Rather, be focused on higher consciousness. I don't have any need for material things. Nor, do the laws of karma bind me. I'm free, without any karmic restraints. I don't get a reward for providing you with this information. Instead, I delight in helping to liberate souls.

I don't like suffering. However suffering reminds me of the work I need to do to help people. Liberating individuals from their suffering is my primary motivation. Of course, the reasons for suffering are as personal and varied as one's voice or thoughts. Humankind needs to understand that suffering is often *accepted* because of higher reasons. No one is a victim," insists Kuan Yin.

"I'm seeing layers and layers, coat upon coat of denseness," depicts Lena. "This is the human condition. It is similar to the hundred thousand lenses comprising a bee's compound eye."

(Bees and humans have very different mechanisms for perceiving reality. The fact that each human perceives through a separate set of eyes as well as other separate sensory equipment assures each person's perception of reality will be quite unique. Theories of Relativism and Paradox are ostensibly accepted scientific conventions. Such theories state that during a scientific observation or experiment, the observer's spatial position and sensory limitations dramatically affect what is experienced about the event. This conversation will once again become relevant during Kuan Yin's discussion concerning levels of existence and Evolutionary Potentials.)

"Some scientists, such as Einstein, are very spiritual. They have already begun to explore and understand this approach to reality," expounds Kuan Yin.

"Kuan Yin is showing me a Middle Eastern woman who is crying. I see layers and layers of, not mist, but like different shades of thick and gooey gray lacquer. I see layers of murky stripes, smoky and jellylike. They have been clinging to this woman for hundreds of years."

"Underneath all of these layers is the woman's pure soul essence: that part of her which knows the processes it will take for her to be released from her karma, that part of her which knows *everything*," continues Kuan Yin. "This is the element of self which *agrees* to suffering and which knows the woman cannot be destroyed. And though this woman's reality may look unjust some 'unjust' bomb cannot blow her up. It cannot destroy her essence, her core being."

"I want to ask Kuan Yin about how to get to another [spiritual] level in order to satisfy something that is missing in my life," states Lena. "Part of me desires to just worship and adore Kuan Yin: to play in the garden and do my artwork. Another part of me feels an urgency to complete school and continue working. Beauty, poetry and spirituality versus analysis and study! What is the point for me to continue pursuing the analytical, when the other pursuits make me so happy?"

"The event that definitely affected your spirit was 9/11. You were more appalled by certain reactions afterward, plagued by the fear that the United States was perhaps moving away from being a conscious and progressive nation. 'I'd better pay attention' was a good first response. The very reasons that make you, Lena and Hope, come to me for these sessions are the very reasons that made you concerned about the welfare of your country," responds Kuan Yin.

"Kuan Yin is showing me a slide show, very quick, successive pictures of Buddhist Monks. I don't know if they are actual human beings or hypothetical. I think Kuan Yin is trying to tell me that whether one devotes one's life to Buddhism or any other kind of worship; it doesn't guarantee one's thoughts are continually on God. They're thoughts could just as easily be focused on playing soccer or meeting a pretty girl. Kuan Yin is saying that no matter which path I choose, I always have the opportunity to focus my thoughts on Her.

I didn't expect Kuan Yin to come back so quickly with such a clear answer. It's been a very serious concern of mine for quite awhile. What is so interesting is that usually there is a bit of a lull in her response. It takes awhile for her to respond with an answer. However, not this time. For some reason, I keep seeing many visuals: mostly flowers or plants. I wonder why she is now showing me so many 'rapid-fire' visuals of flowers and plants?

I remember how she talked about just being with a flower. She's looking at the stamen of a tulip right now. I notice, also, that when she's about to leave me, she always quickly gives me something, either a gift or something to think about for our next time together."

"Just let the mind go and look at a flower," instructs Kuan Yin. "Clear your mind. Have more tea parties with cookies. Hope has good insights and dreams. She should therefore record her insights and always trust in her own interpretations. There are multiple meanings to everything," ends Kuan Yin.

Commentary: The Inner Light: My Dream About Core (Soul) Essence

Hearing Kuan Yin's explanation of Core (Soul) Essence, I suddenly understood a dream I'd experienced years earlier. In the dream, an individual I'd known quite well while growing up was behaving in a threatening way. Considered a bully throughout most of his life, his words and demeanor betrayed inner turmoil and a sense of inadequacy. Finally confronting him in the dream, I asked, "Why must you behave like this?"

Quite unexpectedly, this simple question triggered a complex and mysterious series of events. Feeling myself 'traveling' through his forehead; clouds and mist surrounding his soul essence, I continued to penetrate thick layers of confusion and anger. Seeing a beautiful and bright light ahead, I intuited that this light represented his truest self. I came to realize that this supposed 'lost soul' was not only not lost, but divine. My dream illustrated that at the center of each person's karmic layers is divinity and oneness. From this dream, I gleaned that it isn't helpful to have pity upon others. Rather, seeing and acknowledging another's divinity from one's place of power; having true compassion; helps others realize their own truth. In retrospect, I cannot help but wonder if this had been yet another dream sent by Kuan Yin.

Though seemingly an irresolvable relationship, I'd now found something positive to focus upon when projecting about this person. And in performing this "compassion for the untruth", I also experienced the positive amplification of my own vibration.

Thus, we can choose to refrain from belittling others or ourselves and to not believe that humanity is primarily competitive by nature. We always have the opportunity to acknowledge the compassionate and loving deeds of others as well as ourselves. It's similar to laughing and then your entire body convulses with joy. Your thoughts and the emotional and physical reaction they engender are one.

Ego naturally prioritizes what it believes to be its most beneficial 'beta' (outer) information. Its unique positioning in the seamless expanse of consciousness demands that it also primarily focus upon helpful *inner* sense data. Even when filtering out detrimental inner sense data, Self may unexpectedly discover 'pearls' buried beneath any layers of discontent and limitation.

19
The Power of Good Intention

August 13, 2004: "Kuan Yin believes that praying for other's well-being is the most incredible thing a person can do. There is something else. Because Kuan Yin is made of pure intention, she *is energized* by the good intention and prayers of people."
-Lena Lees

*L*ena and I began the session today by discussing how it is sometimes challenging for her to interpret Kuan Yin's 'non-linear language'. In the introduction, I mention how interpreting content from the alpha brainwave periodicity can present challenges because its unique format (often metaphor and imagery) requires experience navigating the non-linear realms. Therefore, one must possess specific skills so to process the raw information into a linear context. These skills allow the adept to extract meaningful information from what might otherwise be perceived (by those less versed in the art) as a confusing hodgepodge. Delivery pace and quality can vary from one person to the next. Some individuals are quite verbose, while others remain silent throughout the entire trance, immersed in the constantly changing images and sensations. In the following passage, Lena sheds light on her own unique process:

"It is primarily images and metaphor that I must form into whole sentences. Sometimes I don't understand how I am able to speak full phrases, full sentences set forth by Kuan Yin."

Now, counted down (from 10 to 0), Lena immediately begins to speak from her trance state:

"At about the middle of the countdown, I felt myself in the midst of a lava flow. The very hot lava suddenly turned into rushing water that went down a hole in the earth. I'm just going to follow what is happening here for a moment. My son Michael is here with me. We're both tumbling down what seems like a very scary roller-coaster ride in a tunnel. Tossed to and fro, we're being thrown everywhere. I feel Kuan Yin's presence.

Watching Michael and I experience this tremendous turbulence, she tells me that this is but another process we're going through."

"You're in a tube, being thrown everywhere, experiencing this trauma, because your life sometimes feels like this," begins Kuan Yin. "What you're experiencing in trance right now is what you're feeling emotionally inside."

"I'm going to be silent, for a moment," whispers Lena. "Kuan Yin is showing me something important regarding my son's and my relationship. When I connect with him, I feel an enormous sense of loss. I'm seeing him in layers now. I see how the outside layer, his 'present' physical and emotional needs, is being taken care of. However, his inner core, karmic debt, is still in turmoil. It goes back to his parents, no even beyond. It goes back to his grandparents and even fans out beyond them. There are so many people, souls, tugging on him."

"He is like all humans," asserts Kuan Yin. "You come into the world with layers. You can get caught up in your own and other's layers of karma as well.

Michael is scattered because he is living two lives. When he is asleep his dreams are about his karma. Sleeping and dreaming are also times for karmic healing. During his waking hours, he sometimes gets so distracted that he doesn't even hear your voice. This is because he's still living out his karma. Please do not feel guilty if you cannot always reach him, Lena. You and Michael are on this roller coaster together."

"Now I understand that the reason Kuan Yin is explaining to me the nature of Michael's and my relationship is because we are very connected. I'm seeing an actual magnetic field; a strong magnetic field attracting Michael and I to each other. When I first met Michael at the adoption agency, I said to myself, 'I can't let him go.' I experienced knowingness, an instant recognition; that part of him was me and part of me was him. I'm now hearing Kuan Yin say, 'It's supposed to be this way.'

She's holding out her hands. In her hands she holds a glowing golden rock. It is wondrous how much it radiates energy, heat. She's showing it to me but I don't know what it represents. Before she gave me the huge diamond and now she's showing me this beautiful golden rock.

I'm still in the cave, moving through tubes of dirt. I feel as though I'm in a whirlpool of energy. I don't know how to explain it. I'm going to a place in time when I was very young. It's a place of confidence and power. It's a place where life was so new and magical. Perhaps I'm here because this place in time represents Michael's viewpoint of the world.

I'm just wondering what my life would have been like without all the violence. What would my life have been like if I'd continued thinking, *believing* as I did as a very young child? I'm seeing myself there, listening to conversations between the trees. (As a child, I really could hear the trees talking to one another.) I think I am about four years old.

There was a joke in my family about the time I was riding in my go-cart and bumped into the cherry tree. I cried and cried until my mother came and put a band-aide on the tree. I talked to the trees. They were my friends. I especially love the Eastern Maple trees. We had many growing near the house where I grew up.

Though my family quarreled, I recall the special moments. Once, although my mother was very busy working and raising three children, she took time to place a birdhouse in a favorite tree of mine. And even though each day was a struggle for her, she tried to maintain a garden in the yard. She tried to make things pleasant amidst an environment of chaos and fear. Now Kuan Yin is reminding me to continue to work on my fear. She's reminding me of that magical power I had as a child (and still do have), that this is my *Authentic Self*."

"This Authentic Self is the part of you that lives before and after this lifetime, that is eternal," explains Kuan Yin.

"Maybe, continues Lena, "I'm getting this information because Michael is eight years old and I saw myself in those former images at the age of eight. Kids are so open. They see things in a way that perhaps our eyes have become dulled to. There hearts too are so open. They're easy to give love to. Now, Kuan Yin is explaining how to work with the chakras. *(The word "chakra" can refer to certain traditional systems identifying and describing what are sometimes believed to be the body's primary energy centers or "wheels". This belief has evolved to usually include seven vortices: the "crown", "third eye", "throat", "heart", "solar plexus" as well as the two lower chakras.)*

She's showing me how I can place my hand on my children's hearts when they're resting or sleeping and how this kind of balancing the chakras, can help to make them strong."

"The trauma of everyday living can cause the chakras to get shoved around, disconnected. When resting, one may benefit from light touches to the heart, stomach and head, connecting the chakras to one another and also from the inside out," continues Kuan Yin. "Life is so intense. It can scatter one's energy."

"Kuan Yin believes children are so important for it is they who become the future," continues Lena. "She thinks I did well raising my oldest daughter Lydia; that her chakras are quite connected. That is why she is so functional. Kuan Yin is also mentioning how other adolescents can be so torn, imbalanced; either 'stuck' in their stomachs or lower chakras. I wonder if such imbalances are the cause of chronic eating and other eating disorders."

"When there is so much pain in the heart it naturally migrates to the stomach," explains Kuan Yin. "The pain goes to the stomach because the navel, and all that it represents; maternal comfort and nurturing, is there. In fact, this pain is stored in the stomach until the issues causing the pain are finally resolved."

Lena mentions from her trance, how she sometimes experiences fear in her throat and heart: how she, too, has ongoing stomach issues. Explaining further, she discusses some of her adopted son's emotional and physical issues:

"Michael holds so much grief. From early on, we knew (from his adoption papers) that he had a lot of health issues due to his premature birth. He had pulmonary lung failure as a baby because the lungs are the last area to develop in the fetus. He intuitively knows what he needs. But he needs assistance with his head especially. Help him, Kuan Yin, to connect at the head level and in his life."

"Certain body types can correlate with specific emotional issues," responds Kuan Yin. "For instance, those who are overweight often crave nurturing and motherly love. While all need nurturing, those who are obese may have a greater karmic need and, in some cases, could have lost their mother in a past life. Over-eating can be an attempt by the individual to replace the nurturance of the umbilical cord. For some, it may be that they were not nursed long enough or at all. For others, it could be that they were separated from their mothers too soon.

The mother was not necessarily at fault. Instead, the circumstances surrounding the child's upbringing did not meet the nurturing needs of that particular individual.

In this world, the mothering element is not valued enough. If motherly love were more valued within your society, there would likely be less obesity. Look at your welfare subsistence programs. Women are frequently expected to shoulder the entire responsibility for being single and a parent. And 'Aide to Families with Dependent Children' is oftentimes the first to receive the budget ax.

When individuals and society don't perceive the mother as important, there will always be, as a result, a disproportionate amount of obesity and stomach problems. Here, I want to stress that the stomach, not the heart, is the center of our beings. Some might believe because love and emotions spring from the heart, that it is the heart that directs (and is at the center of) our lives.

However, it is important to remember that it is the stomach which defines our energy field and our identity—everything. Think of those societies, tribes, where a large stomach denotes wealth and power. It is no accident. You identify yourselves through your stomachs. However, because of how your culture holds motherhood in low esteem, your culture is out of balance."

"I wonder if that tube Michael and I were tumbling round and round in represented the intestines," Lena suddenly asks.

"It was a metaphor demonstrating that the 'stomach area of life' is extremely sensitive to trauma," Kuan Yin quickly answers. "It is, in fact, where one 'holds' despair. That's the way you and Michael feel about life: that it's a roller coaster."

(Contemplating Kuan Yin's words, Lena pauses for a moment's rest. As Kuan Yin mentioned in the previous chapter that she welcomed my insights, I had prepared a specific question that now seemed apropos for a discussion on "areas of life". Well into my writing on consciousness and the EEG brainwave frequencies, I was curious to know the spiritual purpose, if any, for humans having five specific ranges corresponding to five complex human behaviors. Inquiring of Lena if this is an appropriate time to ask my question, I here her now affirm that my question is welcome.)

"I heard simultaneously when you asked the question about the brainwave frequency ranges, Kuan Yin responding over your question. At the moment of your question, Kuan Yin had said, 'you mean *defenses*, the layers you take to proceed to the soul'".

"We have," continues Kuan Yin, "at least five brainwave frequency ranges for our survival. They are the built-in defenses of human consciousness. They, similar to the layers, *auras* around the body) represent layers of consciousness."

"Kuan Yin is showing me the layers of density on our planet," continues Lena. "They can be compared to the layers (of energy, karma) coating our bodies. The various brainwaves help us to go beyond, *under* the layers of karma. She is showing me radio waves and microwaves. There are all kinds of waves all of the time. The human brain can access certain waves at certain times."

Taking notes, I recalled the story of a friend whose daughter survived the Loma Prieta earthquake. Mentioning how her daughter found herself, following the catastrophe, commiserating with a group of homeless bats, the mother had marveled at her daughter's composure during the entire ordeal.

Uprooted from their abandoned-building home nearby and disoriented by the intense magnetic waves emanating from the center of the earth, the bat's sonar apparatus was temporarily out of commission. With sporadic fits and starts, trying desperately to navigate up and away, the bats remained in their disoriented state for a long period of time, flying any which-way and sometimes crashing into one another.

"These brainwaves serve as protective elements, helping our human bodies function and survive on this earth plane," continues Lena. "I'm reminded of the theory of the 'skin-encapsulated ego'. Kuan Yin emphasizes, however, that this discussion involves the soul. Gravity holds our physical bodies in place. Our skin holds the spirit in place. Heavy layers of energy, karma (around the earth and the body) weigh us down."

"Every layer is different. The (brain periodicity) waves represent the different layers of consciousness," emphasizes Kuan Yin.

"I'm seeing," states Lena, "each brainwave as a sort of gelatinous substance, layer upon layer; much like the onion skin metaphor. Accessing a certain layer avails one of certain abilities, i.e. trance skills in the alpha range, dream lucidity in the theta range, etc. They all work together perfectly. Kuan Yin is telling me that when an individual 'hits' a certain layer, she or he can heal certain issues."

"Yes," enjoins Kuan Yin. "All the brainwave periodicities work well together on the earth plain for purposes of survival. Instinct 'kicks in' when one's survival is at stake. In the alternative brainwave periodicities (and also in the chakras), many issues can be healed.

Hope, you're really onto something. There will be more understanding of the brainwave frequency ranges. Discovery of even more [alternate brainwave] capabilities, will add to an ever-greater understanding of human consciousness."

"Kuan Yin is feeling very strong today. I've been recovering from surgery and not feeling too well. Help me, Kuan Yin, do the best that I can. I'm having a difficult time. I've been feeling sick, vulnerable and sad. Help me get through it all!

Kuan Yin is wrapped around you, Hope. She's holding you, *embracing* you with love. She's made up of pure intention. You know, Hope, how she is called the 'goddess of compassion and mercy'?"

"Yes."

"She believes that praying for others' well-being is the most amazing thing a person can do. And there is something else. I do not quite understand this concept completely. Oh, I understand now. Because Kuan Yin is made of pure intention, she is *energized* by the good intention and prayers of people."

Commentary: Powerful Magnetic Fields of Attraction

Sometimes overwhelmed by specific cultural systems discouraging a natural inclination to take control of one's life, there is never really an abdication of one's innate power. Even when believing that personal or mass glory or missteps somehow originate from external sources, one is choosing a specific path and therefore, as Kuan Yin states, is in complete control.

Through her morphing, Kuan Yin emphasizes how it is unnatural for our lives to be hopelessly encumbered. Endowed with the potential to re-envision and reform, we travel a self-attracted path.

According to Kuan Yin, personal tendencies are primarily karmic; influenced by parallel beliefs, intentions and emotions. One has the opportunity to break free from any limiting karmic cycles that could potentially keep one stuck in first or second 'gear'. This is why Kuan Yin stresses that waking reality is our "escape hatch", our way out of any limiting patterns. Each of us living an earthly incarnation has an opportunity to develop our full humanity; expanding our aura of love and compassion.

Electromagnetic layers of light and sound can coalesce into massive energy formations such as those witnessed by Ms. Lees: *"Kuan Yin is demonstrating how powerful loving kindness can be: that it can disintegrate even the darkest of energies."*

My epiphany of the power of loving-kindness came in a dream wherein I saw an opening through what was ordinarily, in waking reality, a ceiling. Peering through this cosmic window, I spied a blazing sky of undulating shapes and colors: the infinite love of the universe.

The energy supporting all ego and non-ego dramas emanates out from one's Soul (Core) Essence. One's personal creative force, in turn, magnetizes-in groupings of energetically comparable potentials. Whether beneficial or harmful, they naturally congeal into holographic layers. As the energies between these groupings are synergistic, they will spontaneously attract or repel both interior and exterior reality-parameters. Prime examples of beleaguered and detrimental circular beliefs that can endlessly volley back and forth sometimes for lifetimes without resolution; are "not enough", "better than" and survival of the fittest".

Of course, beliefs and intentions of loving kindness and generosity also reinforce each other. By now, it should be evident that we are constantly engaged in building vibration 'structures'. While perhaps not consciously aware of the attracting power of intention, entire cultures can persist in maintaining the status quo *geometric windows of opportunity* (or oppression). As each window has durability, transcending time and space, Kuan Yin recommends a patient and meticulous approach, allowing one's personal level of intuitive *engineering skills* to fully unfold.

Desire for control is right and natural: stemming from one's driving force to fully experience free will. Such a powerful drive is part of the greater *Authentic Self*. If we falter or if our awareness becomes too constrained, it will be there to catch us, reminding us of our magnanimous capabilities through the vehicle of lucid dreams or trance. Such complex psychic events (awareness) cannot be fully comprehended without acceptance that within each of us is a *spiritual* brain-mind and soul connection.

20
Spiritual Liberation

August 20, 2004: "Whenever an event occurs there is a 'planetary imprint'. Energies are drawn to that imprint. Similar energies are then drawn to the existing energies. The energies that are here on earth have free will."
-*Kuan Yin*

Meeting again this week with Lena, she mentioned she'd been frustrated by her attempts to schedule appointments to complete her field study. So, after completing the hypnosis countdown and witnessing Lena's arrival at her sacred place, I was not at all surprised by the thrust of this week's questions:

"Yes, I'm here with Kuan Yin once again," Lena murmurs, soon after the countdown is complete. "I'm just noticing her garments: how, filled with the usual intricate folds, they are thick, almost uncomfortable. I don't quite understand what the thickness means. I see that Kuan Yin is sitting peacefully. However, she's so wrapped up—it's as if she's swaddled. I'm going to sit and wait for her to tell me what her countenance means. I hear Kuan Yin acknowledge that she knows the struggle I'm going through to keep my life together. I'm asking her, 'What can I do?'"

"You're *doing* it," Kuan Yin reassures Lena.

"I'm still observing the very intricate folds of her robe and wondering what their purpose is. Now, I hear Kuan Yin speak to me. She wants to tell a story of how one can carry the abuse (and shock from that abuse) from childhood into one's present-day relationships. I think she is also telling me, I'm all bound up.

Now her garments are loosening a bit. She's telling me that it can be problematic trying to protect someone or free someone by using your voice to access a person's heart. She's holding a baby, poised perfectly on a lotus. As Kuan Yin is so tightly bound into this form, I believe she's trying to demonstrate something to me. Besides, this person really doesn't look like her, right now. I think she looks like *me*."

"Trying to protect someone else by not speaking your mind isn't very saintly," Kuan Yin suddenly says. "Not expressing yourself, worrying about other's feelings doesn't automatically mean you are being peaceful and tolerant. I'm trying to lead you to something, but you don't quite trust me. I'm trying to lead you to your life path. Please don't be afraid of making mistakes. In fact, no step can be a 'misstep'."

"I see now what she is talking about. It's that perfectionist thing I have. It's as if I'm blocking her today. I've been trying to do my field study, make appointments. Kuan Yin is drawing me there, really *forcing* me to go to San Francisco. I've really been having difficulty getting anything set up. She's telling me she helped me get the one appointment next week. It will lead to a chain of excellent connections for me. It was no accident."

"I just have to get you there to show you what the diamond means. There are many facets to this mystery," Kuan Yin reveals.

"I have to get you out of this stuck place; that place in your heart. Even though the conversation today doesn't look like it should, I need to get you up to San Francisco for you to understand certain elements about the book."

"Kuan Yin thinks my sense of time is humorous," mentions Lena.

"The sense of time in one world is not the same as in another world," informs Kuan Yin. "I'm taking Lena up to San Francisco under the auspices of one plan while another is in the making. If you wish to consult a card-reader or a psychic…"

"I'm suddenly experiencing an *unraveling of my heart*," gasps Lena. "A large piece of the imprisoning cloth I saw earlier is coming free. So in this instance, I guess *unraveling* is a good thing.

I don't know why, but I'm seeing Alcatraz Island and the San Francisco Bay. I'm sensing San Francisco is a very important place for me right now. It will allow me some perspective from my marriage. Kuan Yin is also saying that the meeting I've scheduled there is apparently very important, very personal."

"This is a good time to deal with a lot of your past heartache, your heart congestion," Kuan Yin suggests. "I've been working backwards. First, I took you on a journey of the universe, then to certain countries. After that, I took you to certain states and then where you lived during your childhood. Now, we're back here, in your heart. There are certain spiritual practices that say one is responsible for 'dusting and polishing' the *glass* of one's own heart. Things (blockages) are beginning to unblock, *move* for you. When this happens, there may be deep, uncomfortable pain."

Speaking Kuan Yin's potent words, Lena now has her hand placed protectively over her solar plexus, heart and throat. Writhing in pain, she admits her considerable discomfort.

"It's better to be a conduit. There is stuck energy in the solar plexus, as well. Loosing your voice *{Lena was just healing from laryngitis}* was an opportunity for you to focus on what is locked away in your throat. It's time to examine the 'filter of pain' you've been looking at life through.

"Listen to me," Kuan Yin emphasizes. "The pain in those chakras is there to be felt, experienced. You are going to feel it, the sadness and fear, move. It's part of the 'push-through'. Energy in your solar plexus especially needs to move."

('Push-through' is apparently Kuan Yin's term for a certain healing technique. It appears to be congruent with certain chakra and 'energy work' healing theories claiming that 'stagnant' energy must be transformed or released for genuine healing to occur.)

"I'm both watching and feeling, noticing all of this," responds Lena. "Life is going to feel a little difficult. However, I feel strong enough to deal with this now. I didn't before, but I do now. Kuan Yin is telling me that once I go to San Francisco, I'll understand. It's for the book. I need to get clear for the ending of the book. And for that Kuan Yin says a couple of more things have to happen.

I need to go to the Bay Area: to integrate what happens there and then come back. Only then will things become apparent. Kuan Yin wants me to review the past chapters, as well. She says that one's chosen path and patterns contribute to creating an agenda. Originally, Kuan Yin didn't have an agenda. Now that we have set a time limit for the book, there is an agenda.

She's telling me it's not always a good time to consult a card-reader or psychic. However, she's saying that now is a good time for this. I need to read the past chapters of this book. Then, if I have any further questions, I should go to a psychic. I think some of this has to do with the meaning of the diamond."

"Once you do that and get any other clarifications you need, I'll be able to move forward and finish the final chapters," informs Kuan Yin.

"It's going to be fine. Because you and Hope have a timeline, there is now a timeline. You were mentioning you might want to include certain spiritual exercises as a part of this book. Balance! Practice! Meditate upon my form! These are three excellent spiritual practices to put my teachings in place. I want people to know you are human, Lena. And that spirituality is a focus, a commitment, not a punishment. It's liberating.

This book is for all the people who feel left behind, who don't believe they measure up. I want my readers to see Lena, and to understand how any little thing they do (so to focus upon spirituality) is important," explains Kuan Yin.

Realizing Kuan Yin was trying to get her back on course, Lena was experiencing some fatigue at this point in the discussion. I asked her, and Kuan Yin, if it would be all right if I asked a question. I can't remember my exact wording. And for some unexplained reason, the tape recorder wasn't working towards the end of the session. I remember, though, my query had something to do with karmic "turning points" on the earth. Lena and Kuan Yin both agreed to answer the question. The following conversation is what transpired:

"Yes, there is planetary karmic build-up. It's nothing the planet did: more like a pattern of energy on the planet," explains Kuan Yin.

"Whenever an event occurs there is a 'planetary imprint'. Energies are drawn to that imprint. Similar energies are then drawn to the existing energies. The energies that are here on earth have free will. When you mix free will you get certain deviants. It's intended to be a planet for this purpose."

Lena is now describing to me how Kuan Yin is showing her an image of a school.

"Yes. Kuan Yin is assuring me that everything is ok because earth represents a certain grade similar to a school, that it's all a grand experiment."

"It's possible to completely recreate this earth," professes Kuan Yin. "You'll destroy yourselves before you destroy the earth. Besides, we're talking in dualities because dualities are built into your language. You may believe that just because there is an absence of good, for example, that evil exists. This is not so. In fact, things are far more intricate. It is not a catastrophe that the earth is dying. Actually, things are right on schedule. Your precious earth cannot be destroyed. Sometimes it just *looks* that way."

"Hope. I see her over there, holding you again," mentions Lena, gradually emerging from her trance.

Commentary: Fear of Death Can Create Kuan Yin's Law of Compassion Setbacks

We are on earth, according to Kuan Yin, to learn and live the Love and Forgiveness Principle and to understand its role in the *spiritualization of matter.* That which is empirical is also spiritual as Kuan Yin so often proclaims.

From a belief in a dualistic universe, however, sprang these stark divisions: life versus death and humanity versus nature. In fact, language is riddled with words and definitions originating from a belief in dualism. Exacerbating this separation from Oneness is, according to this Deity, the current chaotic paradigm. The three unhelpful beliefs coupled with the fear of death attract much of the misery and suffering upon the earth. History has repeatedly demonstrated that when populations are manipulated by fear of death and prejudice: the 'protector' can quickly become the oppressor.

Humanity has not always had such an alienated view towards death. Indeed, Avatars instructed in this area of expertise are abundant in Eastern cultures. Visiting that part of the globe, one quickly becomes immersed in an alternative paradigm: a culture dominated by Gods and Goddesses proclaiming the twin spiritual doctrines of karma and reincarnation. Many Native American cultures also view death as a vital transition into another world.

Through its explanations of Kuan Yin's spiritual teachings and quantum theorems, this work establishes a multifaceted view of the Self. Modern physics provides insights as well as suggesting the multidimensional nature of reality.

Nevertheless, it is this MOMENT; this life we are experiencing right now that reigns supreme. How we live this MOMENT is strongly influenced by what we believe happens after death. If one, for example, believes that this life is their singular opportunity in a physical body, one may have a far more driven and perhaps even anxious approach than those believing in multiple lifetimes. Perhaps if theories espousing the immortality and divinity of Self were honored, history might not be fraught with so much greed and war.

21
Ask and Receive

August 30, 2004: "Somehow you survived because your soul had hope and faith, a deep faith that there was something beyond, a reason for existing. You remembered a life beyond this one. Those on the *other side* (in a higher dimension) love you so much that they strongly helped you to remember that you are beyond mere earthly abuse. Do not choose a way of life that interferes with your goals. These goals have been with you for years, *lifetimes*. You will not be able to forget them."
-*Kuan Yin*

Following Kuan Yin's advice in chapter twenty, Lena went to San Francisco to gain perspective concerning certain difficulties arising in her marriage. Away from her family, alone in her hotel room: she contemplated her life and wept. Now praying to Kuan Yin, seven months following her first channeling of the Deity, Lena was able to (without entering into trance) hear and record Kuan Yin's precious words:

"It is your hearts desire to know what love is," begins Kuan Yin. "Parenting helps you to develop and evolve that profound love. Love with a partner also helps to develop that part of you which needs to evolve. That is why there are so many issues, barriers. There are many books about developing love as a spiritual practice. In a partnership the spiritual practice can be there every single day: Fathomless love, detachment and acceptance! Developing objectiveness and watching as a detached observer—these are the traits that one can work on along the way. I know you want to love and feel passion. You want to experience that which comes with a committed relationship, living as one does in marriage.

Sometimes the passion, the newness can vanish. That original passion and newness has the potential, while seeming to propel the relationship forward, to blind one to the deficiencies of his or her partner. What can these so-called deficiencies show us about ourselves? What should we take and use to help us see and develop ourselves? When is it time to abandon the relationship because it is too painful? Love will keep finding that issue, the one that has you running.

Sometimes it isn't those issues that make one want to leave the relationship. Instead, maybe one or both partners have completed the assignment. Whatever is not finished, however, will be repeated again and again in future relationships. It is the law of karma. Karma does not make any distinction between this life and the next. It repeats and repeats until the soul evolves. It removes the dust, the layers, making free that which was imprisoned.

Lena, I love you, I will always be at your side when you allow yourself to hear me. To fully experience my essence, it will help if you can clear resentments, distractions, and any impure substances (impure food as well as thought) that could congest the auras and chakras.

As Hope has said, I chose you because you are open. How did you become so open? I am sorry to say the pain that you once suffered as a child also destroyed some layers that were important for you to stay grounded and centered in this world. The violence to your soul broke that area open.

You suffered a great deal of pain because you also had no strong spiritual belief system introduced to you by your birth family. You knew you needed to look for spiritual support. However, the only places you could find were religious systems that only caused you more fear and guilt.

Somehow you survived because your soul maintained hope and faith. You possessed a deep faith that there was something beyond the pain, a reason for existing. You remembered a life other than this one. Those on the other side (in a higher dimension) love you so much that they strongly helped you to remember that you are beyond mere earthly abuse.

Go, Lena. Experience and love and discover all that you can," directs Kuan Yin. "Take care of responsibilities while still focusing upon your own destinies, hopes, desires, and passions. Do not choose a way of life that interferes with your goals. These goals have been with you for years, for lifetimes. You will not be able to forget them," concludes Kuan Yin.

***

As Lena's increasingly busy schedule had sometimes impeded her focus during our more recent trance sessions together, she had requested (at the end of the former session) receiving either a longer or more elaborate countdown.

Returning from San Francisco, Lena scheduled her appointment, inquiring about utilizing a different hypnotic format altogether. Agreeing this would not be an official channeling; we discussed the options. Eager to accommodate whatever process would most effectively facilitate Lena's trance, I suggested a chakra countdown.

During such a process, a person (when given specific directives by the practitioner) may progress (while in trance) through a kind of 'mind, body, spirit tour', observing and often experiencing emotions and other sensory input corresponding to specific physical areas such as the throat, heart or stomach. While immersed in such a state, individuals are sometimes also able to describe colors or pictures associated with a particular area of the body.

Occasionally, utilizing such a process, a client could also encounter actual past lives dwelling in the energy vortexes. As Lena has previously studied about energy work and the chakras, she was open and curious as to what such a process might reveal.

Uttering leading and pacing verbiage specifically tailored for such a progression, I first ask Lena to describe the sensations and/or visions she is experiencing as she focuses upon her crown chakra.

Fully focused, Lena begins to describe what she is witnessing:

"I'm seeing a beautiful turquoise color in this part of my body," she relays. "I also see the word 'live', and understand it is associated with my crown chakra."

Continuing on, journeying through her body to her third eye, she states:

"I am now seeing a sort of salmon pink in this energy center. My third eye is almost completely open. I'm realizing that asking for and receiving what I need is an important goal for my life. For a long time one of my greatest needs has been to be seen for who I really am. I see myself very objectively, wholly and feel great excitement and anticipation as I somehow realize that part of my life will involve the study of healing touch and energy work."

Calling upon her spirit to fully come into her body, (her 'open space', as she describes it), Lena experiences, first hand, what Kuan Yin has explained in the text: that being human is an opportunity to bring spirit into all that is material; to indeed "liberate (spiritualize) matter". Acknowledging that she has (in the past) resisted being human, Lena's heightened awareness reveals that when refusing to nurture herself (by not consuming the appropriate foods or getting enough rest etc.) she is displaying an old and familiar pattern. Through this hypnosis process,

Lena is becoming more aware that one of her primary goals in life is to love and nurture herself.

Now focused upon her throat chakra, Lena informs me she is seeing a "sunny, golden color". Fully immersed in that experience she suddenly receives a communication telling her she should "not judge too much". During this segment, she also realizes she is having difficulty in her life knowing "when to speak out and when to be silent":

"I want to be able to stand up for myself. However, I'm hearing someone tell me not to be too attached to the reaction of others, that it can change my original intention."

About to make the suggestion we go to Lena's heart chakra, I suddenly feel discomfort in my lower back. (During hypnosis, past life regression and energy work, I often simultaneously feel energy blockages and other physical sensations experienced by my clients. When this occurs, I realize Spirit could be trying to convey that this is an area of concern for the client, that she or he is 'holding' some kind of energy. Trauma, misunderstanding and limiting beliefs can remain at the cellular level until a waking or dream experience helps to resolve them or until the individual is able to fully process them. Often, the client will not be able to move on from a specific personal issue until the blockage is resolved.)

Taking note of this 'psychic detour', I ask Lena if she, too, is feeling this same, rather pronounced, discomfort. Acknowledging that her lower back is bothering her, Lena is eager to understand, explaining:

"Sometimes I feel cut off, as if my upper body is separate from my lower body. That area feels pretty vulnerable right now," Lena continues. "It's that anatomical location where parents *pat* their children. It can be a comforting or reassuring pat or it can be an authoritarian signal, emphasizing who is in charge. Of course, a pat can also be one step away from a spanking. It feels a little jellylike and dark. I'm having difficulty seeing beyond this stuff," she admits.

Intuiting what should come next, I say, "I think for you to access the source of this discomfort, we should psychically 'drain' off some of the accumulated undesirable energy. It's similar to draining a wound. Remember, this just represents a type of energy. You have the power to hold or release it. It's up to you.

"Yes, I know."

"So when you're ready, just allow the energy you wish to be released today to flow through your body and into your feet."

"I'm releasing it right now."

Then Lena exclaims; "Oh, I see myself there in that chakra now. I'm about ten years old. You know how free that feels; how your body is so new, not as dense as when you get older? I see a sweet, powerful girl. There are so many memories in there. Remember, Hope, how you feel when the creativity just shoots up through your body?

I loved living in the country, connecting with the trees and the soft, furry creatures. When I was young, I could actually understand what the trees were saying. I'm surprised how strong she, my inner child, looks, *feels*."

"Yes, I'm feeling the energy moving up into your entire shoulder area, arms and hands," I respond. "They feel very strong."

"Yes, I feel it too."

"Your inner child really enjoys this connection with you, Lena. She would like it that during those times when you feel overwhelmed by your daily routine, you heed your inner wishes and take a well-deserved rest. We've accomplished a lot for one day. Do you feel complete? Would you like for me to count you back to waking consciousness?"

"I don't feel quite complete. I still have a lot of stomach issues. While I'm still in this deep trance, I would really like to work on them."

"We can do that. I'm tuning in to that third chakra, right now, and it looks to me as if a tightly clenched fist is lodged there. Do you understand?"

"Yes, I see the fist. I *feel* it. It is very uncomfortable."

"I'm sensing that it represents a parallel life. Do you agree? And if so, do you want to continue resolving this today?"

"Yes, I really want to see what this is about."

"I'm feeling some energy movement also occurring in your feet. Remember the technique, how we can observe your feet psychically so to understand what lifetime you're experiencing?"

"Yes. I see a young boy, maybe around eight or ten. He's asking for food. He is desperate to feed himself and his family. It's dusty, desolate all around. I think this is taking place somewhere in the Mid East. However, I don't know exactly where. The youngster's mother and the other women can't go outside."

"What's preventing them from going outside?"

"It's something to do with their religion. So he's the only one who can beg. I'm feeling his hunger, his *starvation*."

"I feel it too. I'm suddenly very hungry and my stomach aches," I confess.

"I don't know if he makes it. I'm feeling so faint from hunger. Now, I'm passing out. I think the boy finally dies," Lena observes.

Pausing for a moment, I ask:

"Does the clenched fist represent the "not enough" belief Kuan Yin has mentioned so often throughout the text; the belief there are not enough resources?"

"I'm not sure. This starvation lifetime seems to be about some kind of karma: that I was very wealthy, greedy and lustful in another life. As a balance, I had to experience the impoverished lifetime."

"But isn't it the same? Isn't the fist just as tightly closed when you describe the details of your wealthy lifetime? That's what I'm sensing."

"Yes. I'm feeling it. The fist is still clenched tightly," replies Lena.

"In a lifetime of abundance, then, hording of what one believes is 'not enough' can occur just as surely as during an impoverished lifetime. Don't these two extreme lifetimes represent opposite sides of the same belief 'coin': the inevitable suffering greed and selfishness can engender?"

"It feels that way in my stomach."

"Are you able to relax the fist and let go; trusting that there is abundance, enough resources upon the earth for everyone?"

"Yes, I'm feeling the fist loosen its grip. It is now an open and relaxed hand."

Commentary: Ask and Receive: Goals That Have Been With Us for Lifetimes

Exhaustion in the cells can occur when cellular systems are overloaded with artificial guilt and burdens generated by limiting beliefs. This is the foremost reason behind cultivating those beliefs and emotions antithetical to "not enough", "better than" and "survival of the fittest". Indeed, I once experienced in a dream a clear correlation between mind and body. Each time I had a stressful thought, I became aware of my leg muscles automatically tightening. This physical reaction became so uncomfortable that it eventually awakened me from a deep slumber.

In the above parallel-life regression, Lena encountered entrapping and polarized realities of impoverishment versus possessiveness. Her experience demonstrates how beliefs of "not enough" and "better than" (and the stress and imbalance they can generate) have the potential to straddle and influence multiple lifetimes in a limiting way.

Kuan Yin wants us to ask and receive: to release any limiting beliefs about abundance. One's 'clenched fist' relaxed, (trusting in love, abundance), one may then cultivate a truly receptive mode. We need to practice completely and gracefully receiving so that when a miracle does come along, we'll be able to first recognize and then effectively assimilate it.

A panacea for any limiting beliefs, the diamond (Kuan Yin presented during an earlier session) represents all forms of abundance and clarity: the antithesis of the "not enough" or "better than" mindsets. Not some forced, over-arching strategy, it is rather the allowing of the most potent force in the universe, loving-kindness to saturate one's aura. Because of its inherently expansive vibration, perfecting this approach offers ultimate transcendence of cyclic greed and disappointment.

22
"Remember the Possibilities"

September 9, 2004: "Don't limit the brightness. Reach through the dark energy and grab it. You might see the smoke coming out of the chimney and you'll even see the smoky sky. You need to reach through the smoke and bring the light to you. Remember the possibilities of something greater than is right here."
-Kuan Yin

*C*ontinuing from our last trance session, Lena agreed upon experiencing a 'chakra countdown': the process of evaluating the condition of one's energy centers. So instead of the standard ten to zero hypnotic approach, we again traveled down from Lena's crown chakra to her solar plexus. Noting the color and vibrancy of each chakra, Lena also practiced expanding and contracting each "chakra wheel", experimenting and becoming familiar with her corresponding comfort level for each energy center.

(It is interesting to note how some may remain too 'open' while others can be too 'closed' in especially their heart and solar plexus chakras during daily interactions. Testing one's chakra comfort level is one way to evaluate whether one is too psychically or emotionally open or closed. In fact, Kuan Yin has mentioned, in earlier chapters, the possibility for being "too open": that improper chakra alignment can perhaps lead to emotional and even physical damage.

Too vulnerable in one's heart chakra or too shielded in one's solar plexus! Psychically 'scanning' one's energy centers, an individual could discover any number of (body-mind-soul) misalignments. It may therefore prove essential to determine and maintain a personal chakra comfort level.)

When eventually reaching her heart chakra, Lena noticed beautiful white billowy clouds against a picture perfect blue sky. Moving on, she found herself immersed in some profound healing process within her solar plexus area, experiencing and exploring layers of damaged tissue. Somewhere during this entire process she became aware of Kuan Yin's presence:

"Yes, she's here with me, now. I've been away from her for a while so I didn't know if she would be here. However, she's like *vroom*, right in front of me and really present: really real. Kuan Yin is today presenting herself as a middle age woman, wrapped in white. She's standing near me and holding a smoky quartz crystal. I don't recall what smoky quartz stands for. All I know is she doesn't doubt me."

"Don't doubt your intuition or take in other's opinion of you. Don't feel bad or analyze the situation too much. Just trust yourself," informs Kuan Yin.

"Kuan Yin is standing up for me, protecting me," Lena's voice drifts off.

"I just want you to get what you deserve. Even if it is just one little thing," consoles Kuan Yin.

"I got off course for awhile. I followed what friends and others wanted me to do instead of listening to my inner guidance," explains Lena. "Kuan Yin is just saying that valuing other's opinions and interpretations can dilute the magic."

"Let the magic happen. It is always there. Abundance and love are always there. Believe in the highest good," proclaims Kuan Yin. "There is a higher essence to everything. The realm you're in has a heaviness that mutes energy. You can penetrate through it, no matter how dark and heavy. Sometimes it has nothing to do with karma. Just don't forget to keep it open. Don't get too bogged down. Don't limit the brightness. Reach through the dark energy and grab it. You might see the smoke coming out of the chimney and you'll even see the smoky sky. You need to reach through the smoke and bring the light to you. Remember the possibilities of something greater than is right here. Be willing to go to the lightness," states Kuan Yin. "Do not feed off what is not right in the world."

"The diamond is what Kuan Yin wants to give to me. It is for personal reasons," Lena says.

"Prosperity can happen at any time," assures Kuan Yin. "I want to give you everything that you need. Focus on that symbol (the diamond) of prosperity. Taking that first step is what you need. Hope too, say and believe that more and more you can have all the possibilities. It is your mantra. I want you both to believe and be open to receiving. Maybe you can imagine a crystal in the place of a real diamond. Focus upon it and imagine what it represents (its energy) to those areas of the body that need healing.

Practice the meditation of seeing me holding and giving you this huge, chunky diamond. Remember (from our previous session) this diamond doesn't just represent material wealth. Its myriad facets also represent consciousness, love and all other forms of abundance. Practice receiving it," instructs Kuan Yin. "Here, it's yours. Just take it."

"OK Kuan Yin, I accept it," replies Lena.

"Remember when accepting this gift, you're equal to everyone else, you're no different. At the same time you're equal to others, you need to also know that you're special, unique. Each person has his or her own uniqueness while also being equal to the next person. Just please accept the diamond. I've been trying to give it to you for years. Of course, there were different circumstances, different needs. I always have tried to give you this."

"I'm experiencing this really large, strong and grounded embodied image of Kuan Yin," exclaims Lena, speaking intently from her trance.

"I wonder if during this short interlude, whether it would be ok to ask a question about counterparts, our mirror selves in our dreams," I interject. *(This seemed like an opportune time as Kuan Yin had just suggested a specific form of chakra work—accepting within, the energy of the diamond. Indeed, counterparts and chakras are closely related.)*

"Yes, you're entirely correct about the counterparts. Hypnosis is a really powerful tool for healing and understanding one's counterparts. Your specialties, Hope, include hypnosis and understanding the chakras and counterparts of self. Another way of understanding counterparts is that they are the personas and emotions coming from the different organs of the body.

For any person, a certain body organ can be the source of nightmares. Each person, of course is unique. A person might mention they've experienced a nightmare. The nightmare may be trying to inform the person that the associated organ needs particular nutrients, elements.

As we've discussed the chakras also need particular nutrients, elements. Certain emotions can also 'live' in the chakras. Limiting emotions can block off certain areas of the body. An individual, then, can utilize these different approaches (hypnosis and/or dream analysis) as a possible preventive medicine: warding off illness in certain prone areas of the body.

I wish someone would do sound tuning of the chakras. Sound comes first in the universe. We're all made of sound."

Kuan Yin then described a computerized device that could measure and adjust the sound vibration for each chakra. She also mentioned that my youngest son, who is an engineer, might want to explore creating such a device.

"It would be like having one's hearing checked. Only one would be working with the energy centers, the chakras. Individuals could get more in touch with their own pulses and their relationship with sound. It would feel really good and could potentially be used for pain management. There will be (in the coming years) a proportionally larger group of the elderly in your society. People will live longer. However, they may have many misalignments in the chakras. Sound therapy could be very soothing as well as help an individual to adjust, to be ready to move on to the next life."

"Kuan Yin is handing me a book with a disk inside and a flower. She's telling me it is time to end the session. She's saying goodbye to both of us. I'm not sure what kind of flower this is. Let me concentrate upon it a little more. It seems to be a combination of a surprise lily and an iris.

The book that I am seeing has rich brown leather binding with intricate gold leaf design. I comprehend how it is a very potent book. I wonder if this is our present book or one from the future. Kuan Yin is telling me, 'Fill it with words'."

Commentary: Vibration Tuning: Developing Your Relationship with Sound

When we are centered and listen carefully, we can attune ourselves to the harmonious and unifying universal tonal resonance. Groups of souls having certain sets of beliefs and corresponding tonal resonance's are magnetized to other groupings with similar vibrations. Strong emotions of love or anger can also contribute to the original vibrational magnetization: *"Whenever an event occurs there is a 'planetary imprint'. Energies are drawn to that imprint. Similar energies are then drawn to the existing energies."* -Kuan Yin

Imagine, for a moment, this earth reality as a school playground for a certain grade level of students. There had to be similarities: magnetizing forces originally drawing the students together in this particular *playground* at this moment in time.

Once in the same vicinity these qualifying students will reform into ever more specialized groups: possibly only interacting with their particular social niche for the remainder of the school year. At one corner of the playground, there might be a group of musically inclined students: on another, a group that is literary-motivated. Located somewhere else in the vicinity of this 'arena' are the athletic students. Obviously, social groupings display a similar vibration dynamic: that without any pretence, like-minded individuals are attracted to other like-minded individuals.

Individuals seeking a deeper level can have life-altering experiences that cause them to eventually coalesce with others seeking deeper answers to a complex world. All of the above examples represent Evolutionary Potential resonances.

You can either continue with your current proclivities or explore new vistas. When sorting out personal vibration data, any individual has infinite options for adopting new beliefs and their tonal resonances. This process is complex. The simplest explanation is that data is automatically absorbed from the conscious mind into the out-of-time minds (such as trance and dreams). These non-sequential mind states also pick up subtle environmental cues. Processing may take minutes or lifetimes, but eventually will render feedback into the conscious mind. The brainstorm that one assumes is instantaneous may, in fact, be the product of a lengthy evolution.

In the out-of-time ranges, time and space appear to *stand still*, or not exist at all, allowing the individual an entirely different kind of experience: a *personal universe* void of time and space. If there were prohibitive associations connected with the original projection, they have the potential to undermine one's present reality. Dreams often reveal whether the individual is being supported or undermined by parallel reality-parameters and their associated vibrations.

23
"Remember Us in Our Beauty & Our Love"

September 10, 2004: "I see all of them: the Twin Tower victims and fallen soldiers of the Iraq War together like a huge sweeping cloud. Now, I'm seeing beautiful blue colors, billowy clouds and hearing the souls say: 'look at us! Look at how powerful we were. Remember our images. We want to be remembered for all the good things. So many people are focused upon revenge and anger. It's the worst thing you can do for those who've passed over. Just remember us in our beauty and our love.'"
-The Spirits

As Lena had many distractions she was coping with in her life, we agreed upon an "extended" hypnotic countdown. Instead of beginning with the number ten, we started with the number fifteen (so to provide her with more time to reach her safe place and then sacred place):

"Yes. I'm here in the bamboo garden. Kuan Yin is very illuminated. Her garment is so bright, so filled with light. She's holding a musical instrument. I think it is a lute. Completely focused upon tuning this instrument—trying to get the sound just right, she does not speak."

"Sit down, Lena, and see what I'm doing," instructs Kuan Yin. "Once this instrument is correctly tuned and kept tuned, any amount of chaos won't matter, won't affect it."

"Of course," maintains Lena, "this is Kuan Yin's metaphor for keeping the body chakras well-tuned. She's telling me this is a continuation of her message (in chapter twenty-two) concerning the effects of sound and vibrations upon physicality. She is also saying that the power of sound (and pulse) is why music is so calming and comforting."

"We've been meeting like this for some months now. I've taken you on these journeys and you know you can return (to normal waking existence) any time you wish. However, I want you to take the diamond, receive all that it stands for. Maybe you can hold a large crystal and imagine it as the diamond. When you place this imaginary diamond on your solar plexus, visualize its potency and value—the highest and safest feelings going into your stomach."

"Kuan Yin is giving me a burgundy or red colored tulip with fringed petals. It is so beautiful," exclaims Lena.

"I want you to bring that light into your body. Practice that," instructs Kuan Yin.

"I'm suddenly seeing myself lying in a thick layer of an oil-like substance," describes Lena. "It is similar to the oil that rises to the top layer of a boiling pot of soup. Above this thick and heavy atmosphere are astonishingly vivid colors of bright light."

"Push it aside. It is like the momentous *parting of the waters*," Kuan Yin instructs. "Only this is parting of dense consciousness. It's the only way to keep you in balance during the difficult times. You know," Kuan Yin concedes, "harder times might be coming. There may be a lot of chaos. People are going to have to (more than ever) rely upon spiritual practice. The only way to remain strong is to pray for others. Don't get too depleted."

"I'm seeing endless light, endless possibilities," exclaims Lena. It is an infinite light that goes on forever. It's amazing. It is so much more powerful than any darkness humans can create.

Kuan Yin is reminding me that she (telepathically) sent me an article on Chinese medicine when I was in the herb store. She wants us to stay alert to the things she sends or puts in the path for us. Now she is giving me some general advice":

"The best thing you can do is to write it down when you comprehend those gifts I've sent to you. One reason you may not take to heart or practice these techniques (that I've presented to you) is that you don't believe that you are valuable. Another is that you don't have enough faith. It's all about faith," emphasizes Kuan Yin.

"Kuan Yin is showing me what looks like a spiral tunnel (where my navel really is). Together, we're going around and around, trying to relax the walls of the tunnel. Now we're going even deeper into my stomach. Kuan Yin is in some deep layer, working on healing and relaxing the tissue. I see a tiny, tiny black pellet, like a tiny seed deep in the tunnel. What is it? What is it made of?

Kuan Yin is placing her form way deep in the seed. This particular form of her is a beautiful, intricately carved and relaxed Kuan Yin. For some reason, right now, something about soldiers is coming up. I'm seeing medals of Honor with white and blue ribbons. I wanted to go to the vigil to honor the fallen soldiers," grieves Lena, still deep in trance.

(This week marked the third anniversary of 9/11 and several local events were being held to honor the fallen. Lena's anguish concerning these tragic national events had clearly affected her at a profound level.)

"I'm so sorry. I have feelings of awful sadness, powerlessness about the deaths of the soldiers and the people who were in the Twin Towers at the time of the bombings. Kuan Yin is standing in front of them. She is saying the soldiers do not want to be remembered as a burden. They're souls want to be appreciated without any accompanying judgment. I want to send them love. I feel so much sorrow," Lena suddenly breaks down, weeping while still in trance.

"All the soldiers' desire is a simple acknowledgement that they died," responds Kuan Yin. "It is the same for the souls who died in the Twin Towers."

"Their greatest sadness is the anger and hate that abounds," Lena continues. "They are all just standing there and saying; 'Why isn't everyone talking about the life we had that was very good?' I see all of them together like a huge sweeping cloud. Now, I'm seeing beautiful blue colors, billowy clouds and hearing the souls say, 'Look at us. Look at how powerful we were! Remember our images. We want to be remembered for all the good things. So many people are focused upon revenge, anger. It's the worst thing you can do for those who've passed over. Just remember us in our beauty and our love.'

I'm remembering a dream I had right after 9/11 about the explosion. It was so deep, so real. Coming from the explosion were all the glorious things that had been a part of these people's lives: beauty, love, giving and creativity.

Kuan Yin is watching all of this as if the entire drama were playing on a TV or movie screen. Neutral, constant, unaffected, she's just there. However, her non-judgment doesn't mean she's heartless or doesn't care."

"Lena, the only way to really utilize your human experience is to practice some kind of meditation or visualization. It does work. People really need it. It's the only way to get through the difficult times."

"I've known about this for a long time, about the benefits of meditation and visualization," confesses Lena. "However, Kuan Yin is reminding me again. She's saying how this kind of practice puts us in the 'Kuan Yin spirit'. You're the *watcher*. Instead of judging, you just see. Whether meditating upon her form or bringing light into the chakras: all of these techniques can help us in our life.

Kuan Yin is telling me (and you, Hope) that it is a really powerful thing to do a meditation that involves surrounding a person with light. The individual (meditated upon) will feel the good intentions and that you want the highest good for her or him. Of course it's also beneficial for the one who is meditating.

It also can be powerful to explore hypnosis and chakra alignment techniques. Letting go (of former limiting beliefs and impressions) and seeing what can be learned about yourself and others helps with compassion."

Here, Lena mentions she wants to ask Kuan Yin about her relationship with her husband:

"I'll just wait for a moment and see if she can tell me anything about a past life or something I need to do to help him. Now, I'm seeing him as a floating ball of energy, about ten years old. All his thoughts, impressions of life keep cycling through him like a looped tape going round and round. These thoughts and impressions have been with him for such a long time that he has created a deeply ingrained loop. Now it's so deep, it is difficult for him to climb out of it.

Lena continues to describe what she is witnessing, saying she senses a specific symbol and/or energy surrounding her husband. The energy is somehow informing Lena that her husband does want to heal. However, each time he sees Lena, it's as if she is wearing a mirror on her chest. He gets irritated at seeing himself.

"Obviously, there is something about this whole situation that is very comforting for him," Kuan Yin continues. "However, you can't always be in charge of helping him. Do you understand the reason that you two are in this dance cycle together?"

"I'm psychically (or somehow) getting the message that I constantly give him a signal that says I can fix him," Lena suddenly realizes.

"Your ego wants to believe you can fix him. Meditate on the fact that you can't fix him," explains Kuan Yin. "What is strong is admitting you are limited, that you can only do so much. You can't do any more than any one else is able to do. You need to say (to yourself and not to him directly) over and over: 'I can't fix you. I can't make it all better.' It's all about 'letting go'."

Suddenly reminiscing, Lena recalls her circumstances as a child:

"My role in the family was to make sure everyone else was emotionally ok. I knew we were just little kids and in order for my parents to take care of us, I'd better help so they could be emotionally and physically ok. I learned very early on that to do this would require me be less than I really am. I'll be powerless. I'll be small, whatever my parents wanted. I didn't want to interfere.

I decided that I needed to make both my parents happy and healthy so they could take care of us children. I'd be anything they want me to be. Ultimately, I gave them all my psychic energy, because I didn't have anything else to give. And because things didn't get much better, I came away from my childhood believing I was weak. But I really want to know something. Does it mean I'm weak if I can't help them or be what they want? That's my issue. I can see it so clearly, now. I realize that I really believe I'm weak if I can't fix people. Is it true, Hope? Am I really weak?"

"Kuan Yin has often commented upon your wonderful capacity for love and compassion and that you have great physical and emotional resilience. By simply letting go, allowing others to make their own discoveries concerning how to attract their optimum reality, I realize I'm honoring their unique path. People have free will. And even if it appears as though they need rescuing, they're really very strong. They need to 'travel their own road of consciousness' in their own way. Remember what Kuan Yin has always said: *'No two paths of liberation look the same.'*"

"I'm really seeing how I can't fix others," concedes Lena. "However, I can pray for them and love them. Even though 'fixing others' is a good intention, Kuan Yin says it is a 'misinformed ability'. It doesn't mean I'm weak if I can't make things better."

"It's a humble mantra," reaffirms Kuan Yin. "Saying, 'I can't fix people', one is no longer coming from an ego point of view."

"Well, Kuan Yin knows I have to go soon. She's showing me her beautiful form, visions of children."

"Come back every day to see me," Kuan Yin bids Lena goodbye.

"Kuan Yin has so much love for people that she won't interfere unless they call upon her for help. Many Easterners know about her, but she is not so well known in the Western hemisphere. She wants to remind Westerners that she is a deity who is very available. They can access her whenever they need to. Unless a person calls upon her, though, she cannot help. She's also saying there are many other deities, not just her."

"To all people everywhere, I'm here and at your service!"

Awakening from her trance, Lena rushed to her desk, trying desperately to recall and record Kuan Yin's words.

"I'm trying very hard to remember what Kuan Yin said today! It would really assist me in my life right now. But it's difficult. It's like waking up and trying to record a dream. Even after just a few seconds, I'm unable to recall her words."

"It's all written here and on tape," I reassured Lena, pointing to my blue notebook. "If you wish, I can type it up and send it to you as an email in a few days."

"That would be very helpful."

Commentary: Tonal Resonance and the Outward Progression of Consciousness

The outward progression of consciousness culminates in the expression of highly individualized electromagnetic impulses: those unique tonal resonances of every living creature. According to Kuan Yin, beliefs, emotions and their corresponding vibrations create specific tonal *values* for individual and group consciousness. These values ultimately attract the reality-parameters of one's life.

Warning that we should be wary of getting hung up in any deeply-ingrained *karmic loops* i.e. limiting belief systems or identities that can be attracted over and over, Kuan Yin's interpretation of how to achieve "the most divine life imaginable" is a proactive as well as interactive process between ego and desired realities. Continuing, she advises that reincarnation is for the purpose of assuming many varying identities and beliefs:

Sojourning through my dream maze, I happened upon the ghostly ruins of a fire-gutted house. Only the basement and surrounding foundation (which I believe represented humanity's innate spiritual tools of free will and loving-kindness) still stood. And although this was a scene of terrible devastation, the hope of rebuilding from the remaining foundation (as humanity's basic spiritual tools can never cease to exist) seemed to be the underlying message. Surveying the scorched earth surrounding the structure, my attention gravitated to six symbols branded in the earth. Intuiting that each represented the soul *pattern vibration* of a deceased family member, the mandalas (shapes having spiritual significance) symbolized deeply ingrained belief loops (personal beliefs and intention) carried from one life to the next.

24
Seasons of Life

September 27, 2004: "There are the waves and there is the wind, seen and unseen forces. Everyone has these same elements in their lives, the seen and unseen, karma and free will. The question is, 'how are you going to handle what you have?'"
-*Kuan Yin*

School was just beginning for Lena's children and it was difficult for her to find time to schedule a session. After a two-week period or so, we were able to meet. Counting Lena down to her sacred place, she once again found herself near the waterfall in the bamboo grove:

"Kuan Yin is here. I am somehow trying to get a sense of myself, where I presently am in my life. Kuan Yin doesn't have any answers for me right now."

"Just present a place representing where you are right now in your life," instructs Kuan Yin. "I'll just let you contemplate, for a moment, where you are in your life."

Sighing, Lena comments, "I'll just be with Kuan Yin's question for a moment. Kuan Yin is reminding me how fickle a sense of time can be."

"Sometimes, we interpret a minute (a moment in time) according to our mood. So, a moment can be happy or fearful or it can contain feelings of not knowing what to do. It's ok not to know what to do," reassures Kuan Yin.

"Just be with it. Just be with the fact that life is always changing but that humans always have the ability to live in the moment. Receiving a psychic reading isn't always the answer. Sometimes things can shift. Something that is true one moment is not necessarily true the next. There are many invested elements: elements that can affect the outcome. Ultimately, the outcome depends upon the individual's free will. Everyone wants to know the outcome, the end.

However, there is no end, only *seasons of life*. We've all heard it said before. Certain events, for example a move or a divorce, can be like a death. There are other examples, of course. Rebirth, flowering, wizening and then dormancy: the springs, summers autumns and winters of our lives represent one's full cycle of seasons…"

"Wait just a minute, Hope!" Lena exclaims. *Silent for only a few moments, Lena begins to speak once again:*

"I'm feeling something in my body. It is some kind of an energy or force. Maybe it will go away. It feels like some kind of interruption. My head, body, even the taste in my mouth is different. It's so strange. I have a big head and a little body, all sorts of unfamiliar sensations. I think it is my daughter, Marina. She's *inside* of me. During this time (season) of *her* life, she seems very frustrated, angry. I'm feeling her frustration right now. Her emotions are very developed. However, she's not able to express them.

I'll ask Kuan Yin to send her some peace and calm. It's not surprising, sometimes she wants to get so close, to be back inside my body."

"When a three-year old is miserable, they may feel as though it will never end," intervenes Kuan Yin. "She will eventually understand that her brain and body grow and evolve, that things are in constant flux and will get better."

"I feel a little less encapsulated by my daughter, now. I'm trying to tell her to calm down. In my moment-to-moment sense of time right now, I'm realizing that this is probably her naptime (at daycare). Hopefully, she can calm down now and take her nap."

"Your daughter gave us a commercial break. You know, Lena, not every decision depends upon you. Your husband has decisions and you have decisions. Karma is involved in decision-making. There is a time to push and a time to let go. Everything in life is like a birth process. A problem can be like a birth: something new can be created from an old problem. It's not so important about the end or resolution of a problem, rather it is how you are with it, how you *interact* with it."

"I'm seeing some kind of visual. Kuan Yin is trying to give me an image of how this all works," describes Lena.

"This 'birthing' is a learning process," asserts Kuan Yin. "This learning process involves constant giving, learning, receiving, responding, interpretation and appreciation. Your husband is learning how to appreciate people instead of things or accomplishments. Careers, accomplishments in one's life tend to be a male emphasis. Women tend to focus upon relationships. Many men are learning from women how to appreciate people versus accomplishments. The universe will bring people anything they want. Sadness is attached to all of this, people not wanting to believe in themselves. Yet, you always find what you need."

"Remember, Hope, how previously, you've asked about certain lost theological texts?" asks Lena

"Eventually the Dead Sea Scrolls were supposedly 'accidentally' discovered," continues Kuan Yin. "Resulting from people wanting to know the truth about such matters, such an important discovery was, indeed, no accident. There are great scholars who've extensively studied these. They understand and would be happy to share this knowledge.

People want what is comfortable for them right now. It's just where they are right now. However, there is continuous evolution of souls. As I've said before, I won't force myself upon anyone who does not want to hear my message. An example might involve someone desiring to be loved. One could cast a magic spell. In the final analysis, wouldn't they rather just want know the person loved them without the spell?"

"I used to believe that meeting one's true love 'across the room' was an impossibility; that it would never work out," Lena enjoins.

"There is so much karma happening all the time. So much, that you probably can't put your faith in methods debunking instant attraction," Kuan Yin responds.

"Too much pragmatism in a relationship is not so good, I guess," agrees Lena.

"Let's see what happens next," comments Kuan Yin. "Not even God knows. Let me restate that. The cool thing about free will is that even if one has a huge bag of karma, there is still a lot of free will for all those souls coming into the world. Stop looking at the half-empty glass. Remember to 'make lemonade from lemons', as the saying goes. Just practice being in the moment! It would be best if you could practice being in this moment and then in the next moment and so on," Kuan Yin instructs Lena.

"Try to be here, right now. Focus upon a leaf fluttering, light reflected on the waves. Things are more beautiful, afterwards. Make it your own experience. Things will taste, feel better. Colors will be brighter and you'll feel more alive. It is the only thing that is real. The past was real, but reliving it or worrying about the future is futile."

"Taking the children for a day at the beach, the other day, I made an effort to savor every moment," Lena recalls. "Focusing upon a leaf fluttering in the wind, I then turned my attention to the breaking waves. Experiencing the moment to moment beauty and joy, I felt more alive, more *real*."

"You can have a hope. However, to agonize over the future is not very skillful," Kuan Yin relays.

"Kuan Yin is showing me picture of a windsurfer skimming effortlessly along the ocean's surface," describes Lena.

"While quite skilled, he is nevertheless very focused on the elements around him. The windsurfer is focused upon how to turn the sail. His question must always be, 'what am I going to do with the wind that is blowing right now,'" instructs Kuan Yin.

"There are the waves and there is the wind, seen and unseen forces. Everyone has these same elements in their lives, the seen and unseen: karma and free will. The question is, 'how are you going to handle what you have?' You are riding the karmic wave underneath and the wind can shift. Everyone must take what they see and deal with that which is unseen. Fall into the *water*!"

Commentary: Invested Elements: Karma and Free Will

Limiting identities can range from believing one is 'above it all' to being totally Machiavellian to a mixture of these two extremes. As Kuan Yin's Law of Compassion dictates, such identities can eventually attract the same. Because of the peculiar nature of the earth environment, all who incarnate here must ultimately master the skill of effectively assimilating raw events and emotions, expressing them in their own individual ways. The earth and its vast and varied environments, offer unique opportunities to gather strength and ingenuity: to actualize the above.

It's natural to want to utilize pre-existing talents and achievements. However, Kuan Yin stresses that over reliance upon 'former' (pre-birth) identities can lead to setbacks. Rather, she wants us to approach each new incarnation as a fresh experience, gleaning all we can from our new acquaintances and surroundings while simultaneously building upon what we already know.

Notice in the above "waves and winds" quote, the emphasis upon 'focus'. Indeed, we are to utilize our focusing capabilities; our attention to best navigate, "the wind that is blowing right now."

Kuan Yin asserts that the written and spoken word could draw or repel expansive and/or limiting personal and mass realities. When a certain percentage of individuals comprehend a given principle, this amassing of vibration can tilt human consciousness in a particular direction. Always available to choose, Kuan Yin's *Love and Forgiveness Principle* offers hope for a new and expansive direction.

Kuan Yin's Law of Compassion Formula

The "waves" of Kuan Yin's "wind and waves" metaphor represent Her Law of Compassion formula. The "w" stands for our expansive (or limited) vibration waves emanating out from an originally created thought/intention/emotion. Innately emitted, these waves continually attract vibrationally-corresponding objects and/or events.

The "a" stands for accelerate/affirm: that when one (either intentionally or by default) faithfully creates a specific concept, it will align with, accelerate and actualize a specific Evolutionary Potential. This can only occur, however, if no conflict with the original thought/intention/emotion wave exists.

"V" is for the velocity (veracity + vitality + vividness= velocity) of a specific idea, intent, word, sound or vision. This aspect of Kuan Yin's law of Compassion equation posits that all ideas, sounds and visions will have strong or weak concept/emanations. For example, veracity represents the truth of a particular idea while vitality represents the strength: its degree of alignment with the universal energy. Vividness, on the other hand, refers to the degree of eternally-abundant love and compassion held in an idea. Fully comprehending this and trusting: one flings wide open, the magnetization gateways. Attracting expansive realities is always within one's realm of possibilities. However, limiting beliefs or feelings of unworthiness could block these realities from being personally realized.

Theoretically, there are only two primary Evolutionary Potential (EP) attraction categories (platforms): worthiness and unworthiness. One or the other can be activated when thoughts, words or actions by the individual and/or external stimuli, (for example, physical or emotional calmness or trauma) excite corresponding neuronal responses. A worthiness EP attraction platform might, for example, include the belief that mankind is good and that one has an abundance of resources. The complimentary emotion to this will most likely be a sense of peace and satisfaction with one's present circumstances.

Conversely, an unworthiness EP attraction platform might include that mankind is flawed and that one does not have access to adequate resources.

Feelings of "not enough" may typically seesaw back and forth between the overcompensating "better than" and "survival of the fittest" beliefs. The resulting emotional component of this EP platform, therefore, can be anxiety accompanied by a strong sense of competition. In either case, these two antithetical platforms will potentially draw or repel similarly attuned cellular and cosmic reality-parameters.

On any given day one will experience vying shades of gray of worthy or unworthy thoughts and emotions. A worthy EP attraction platform could therefore cancel out an unworthy EP attraction platform and vice-versa. On one hand, this process can prevent many unwanted 'unworthy' outcomes. On the other, it may impede any real progress.

Combined, any strong or weak concept/emanations form the degree of velocity (or force) of any thought/intention/emotion. Naturally, certain idea, sound or envisioning velocities will be more aligned with the universal energy and therefore have more power than others.

For example, thought/intention/emotion idea, sound or envisioning velocities aligned with love, compassion and forgiveness will be readily associated with deeply-beneficial, universal potentials. Indeed, directing such beneficial beliefs, words and visions outwardly towards others (accelerated by focused intent) is the action Kuan Yin defines as prayer and also as "the most powerful thing a person can do".

Finally, the "e" stands for what we are constantly attracting: Evolutionary Potentials from All That Exists. $W + a + v = e$. This is the essence of Kuan Yin's Law of Compassion equation. With practice, one can learn to accurately sense and evaluate the velocity of any particular idea, sound or vision. So to attract through ones innate wave dynamic their most abundant Evolutionary Potential, one should faithfully affirm and/or envision what they've determined to be their most expansive thought/intention/emotion concept/emanations.

25
"Be Still & Watch the Spider Build Its Web"

November 16, 2004: "Immerse yourself in the beauty of the world. Begin with marveling at the beauty of nature. Art and music nurture and balance the self. Indulge yourself with every art that engages the senses. Take shelter in the arts. Taste, touch and smell: anything that uses and appeals to the senses! There are, as other examples of creative outlets, the culinary arts and working with flowers."
-Kuan Yin

While we'd talked on the phone and seen each other in passing, because of our hectic schedules it had been a while since Lena and I had met. Agreeing to a more protracted countdown, I began with the number fifteen and slowly began to count backwards, helping Lena to attain her desired trance level:

"Yes. I'm here in my usual place by the bamboo grove and the waterfall," Lena explains. "Today, I can feel the heat and moisture. The air is thick with humidity. I see Kuan Yin and am walking towards her. She is very hopeful and joyous to speak with us once again.

Now, she takes my hands, gently massaging my palms. Intently observing my hands, she remarks upon where I've been and what I've done so far in my life. Both of us now intently scanning the intricate lines crisscrossing my palms; a gateway to other worlds suddenly appears before me."

"Haven't you come a long way from where you've started?" inquires Kuan Yin.

"Yes," agrees Lena.

"Kuan Yin is complimenting me. She says I possess a very important and necessary skill: the ability to navigate difficult times in a positive way."

Continuing to read Lena's palms, Kuan Yin says, "I see you are willing to go as far as you have come. There is a vastness, spanning out before you. Use the power of your accomplishments to propel yourself into the future."

"I'm recalling a TV program about the aftermath of the Vietnam War. It focused on Laos," details Lena. "During the war, bombs that opened up and dispersed thousands of mini-bombs (*bombies*, I think is what they're called) were dropped into fields in that area. Hundreds, maybe thousands of adults and children have been maimed or killed when accidentally detonating these menacing remnants of war.

I have an overwhelming need to go to Laos and to help the people in the villages. I could join with the Mennonites who are already there helping. They have scouts who scope out the fields and then call in the bomb detonators. These volunteers are not just talking about world service they're doing it right now.

Taking my kids to some of the major toy stores is frightening to me. I want them to learn how to be stewards of the earth and live a simple life. The question I have today for Kuan Yin is about choosing options for living. Can you guide me to a service? I'm yearning for something. I'm remembering now how I felt such hopefulness and optimism emanating from Kuan Yin during the countdown."

"It's a perfect Buddhist time," responds Kuan Yin. "Your hopes have been dashed. Your cup has been overturned. Some of the aspects of your life (as well as the recent election) have not gone the way you had hoped. However, some of the stagnant energy has been cleared away. It is time to re-group. Everything is right on schedule."

"Some of my friends, who'd worked very diligently on the election, are very disappointed. They ask me if their campaigning was in vain. Have my friends just wasted their precious time?"

"The outcome is not important," contends Kuan Yin. "What is important is that those who gave their energy and time *seized* the moment. Don't have an attachment to the outcome. Do the right thing because it is the right thing to do, such as helping others, helping the earth."

"Certain friends have spoken about leaving the United States. They are thinking seriously about moving to New Zealand or other foreign shores. They're discouraged about our government and worried about the future. They are actively researching other places to raise their children."

"There is no place to hide," advises Kuan Yin. "All of those existing on the earth are in this together. People can immigrate to those places if they wish. However, it won't release anyone from the collective planetary intention and personal responsibility to others."

"Suddenly, I'm experiencing an image;" Lena relays. "Kuan Yin is showing me a certain symbol. It is of my husband. Kuan Yin is trying to nurture him. In my visualization, he appears as a tiny infant. She is trying to rebirth him. She's telling me it's not up to me to fix him."

"It is not up to you. It is up to the spirit guides," Kuan Yin gently admonishes. "You have to turn it over to them. Stop trying to be a super-being. Turn over your tendency to fix him."

"Kuan Yin says this is a good visualization for letting go, letting it be. We only have the power to help ourselves."

"Some of the media (available in your culture) tend to go after one's emotions. Fear, sadness and anxiety can make money for these interests. When people watch, allowing themselves to be manipulated by such limiting emotions, they feed the 'machine'. Instead, immerse yourself in the beauty of the world. Begin with marveling at the beauty of nature. Art and music nurture and balance the self. Indulge yourself with every art that engages the senses.

Take shelter in the arts. Taste, touch and smell: anything that uses and appeals to the senses! There are, as other examples of creative outlets, the culinary arts and working with flowers.

Some third world countries hold many local festivals. Festivals are joyous. They are a way to celebrate the beauty of the local culture and the camaraderie between the citizens. Participate in local festivals! You have a lot more power and options for creating your world around you than you are now aware of. Don't allow mind *chatter* to bring you down. There is so much opportunity to accomplish things. Sometimes we limit ourselves."

"I'm asking Kuan Yin about the book, what we need to do to complete it."

"Make time to do a final editing of the book. Once you have a good grasp of the material it will open your mind," maintains Kuan Yin. "Gather your questions together. *Meet* me with your questions. Ideas don't just float in the universe; they are linked together, related. If you don't have a thought I can't have an answer.

A physical book delineating my spiritual teachings in the hands of many should likely be very healing and inspirational. Sometimes things take hold slowly at first and then very quickly. Don't be discouraged in the beginning. Sometimes when the content and even the form changes; new opportunities can arise. Your task is to get the book into physical form," instructs Kuan Yin of both Lena and I."

"I'm seeing our book lying on tables. It is purplish blue. Kuan Yin is showing me a map of the British Isles. She's saying her book will be very popular in many of those geographical areas, to begin with. Well, Kuan Yin is saying it's time for her to go. As in previous gatherings, she's leaving us something. It's an image of a little spider in the corner of the room."

"Spiders are patient and meticulous," Kuan Yin professes. "Humans sometimes believe that insects are insignificant because they are small. However, their work is of great importance to the world. Be still and watch the spider building its web."

Commentary: The Shape of Manifestation

Einstein forever redefined the universe as it previously had appeared in Newtonian physics. Within the constraints of his theories, the universe is depicted as infinitely malleable and complex: wherein the time/space continuum acts as a wave pushing reality-parameters towards or away from a given reference point. For purposes of this discussion, the reference point is individual or mass point (s) of intention.

Kuan Yin has revealed a three-dimensional matrix wherein the horizontal lines represent one's unique Points of Intention spectrum and the vertical lines represent multiple probable occurrences.

The lateral (or third) dimension holds mirror-symmetry information of one's original Point of Intention and multiple probable occurrence grid intersections.

Obviously, the infinite locations within this matrix can allow for myriad choices: the power point for the control and energy that you seek for your life.

Focused intent (personal projections plus emotion) could be considered the 'engine': the powerful driving force causing particular Evolutionary Potential Platforms to move closer or farther apart: solidifying or dispersing a reality. As discussed, one's Point of Intention is one's Attraction Point. Well-meaning or harmful intentions and their corresponding impulses can bundle together to create a beneficial or unbeneficial 'package', sparking specific attraction responses. Even a momentary intention can tip the balance, tremendously reshaping your *web of life*.

There are as many probable realities as there are Points of Intention ranging from complete compassion to revenge. Performing pirouettes, a dancer will need to 'spot' a particular corner of the room to avoid dizziness. When you are moving and spinning through your life, you can maintain your balance by focusing only on those *points* you want to keep and develop. To avoid any conflict within this spectrum: to stay 'on point', so to speak, continue affirming and/or visualizing your compassionate intentions. Otherwise, the potentially distracted ego can volley back and forth between bliss and despair and all gradations in between.

Beliefs and emotions are analogous with body mass. When someone has expansive beliefs and emotions, the resulting energy field resonates outward creating a time/space curvature able to pull in reality-parameters mirroring such beneficial emanations. Your mindset, then, sets up the warp, wherein reality-parameters will 'ride' towards you. Becoming stars and galaxies, Kuan Yin adroitly depicts how the dynamic fabric of the universe is indeed an extension of our own consciousness.

26
Kuan Yin & The Elephant

December 14, 2004: "See how I don't have to try too hard. The elephant effortlessly carries me (us) on her back."
-*Kuan Yin*

Although steeped in finals and holiday activities with her family, Lena was able to make time for the following two-hour trance:

"I know it has been about a month since I've visited with Kuan Yin. I've missed not seeing Her. Sometimes, when I feel as if I'm drowning in busyness, I think of her. When I feel like that, I can't help but think of her. I've also been going back and reading some of the chapters. I wanted to follow up on the suggestion Kuan Yin made during the last conversation; that I formulate questions from the material we've covered so far. Remember chapter twenty-one, Hope? We completed that chapter together after I went to San Francisco and saw the beautiful Kuan Yin sculpture."

"Yes. I remember Kuan Yin's suggestions."

"I guess that feels very relevant to me, right now. Kuan Yin spoke of how one can work upon one's dharma through personal relationship. She mentioned how events in a relationship can flow along easily. When they stop flowing, however, there can be a lot of stagnation. The pain I've been experiencing lately occurs when I'm unable to help my husband overcome his unhappiness. It is very difficult to live with someone who can't be content. He's not happy with his job nor is he happy when he's at home.

I wonder what my lesson is. What is my next step? You know how (in the I-Ching), it is said there are times to rest and times to push? I've been wondering what to do next in my marriage. Should I rest or push?"

Stating that she wanted the above question to set the focus for today, Lena requested (as many important issues were weighing upon her mind today) a longer countdown than usual. Upon being counted down from fifteen to zero to her sacred place, Lena immediately begins to laugh with delight:

"I didn't expect Kuan Yin to show up so soon. It's extraordinary! She's perched on top of an elephant:

"I had to come in a different form today, to shake you, get you out of a certain expectation of me."

"She wants me to come along. So I guess I'll just come along: ride on top of this huge elephant. I'm just wondering how I will be able to climb on."

"Don't think like an earthling! Don't analyze every step. Just get on."

"It's kind of a nice sensation. The elephant's body is swaying heavily but gently. I feel its power and yet at the same time there is a softness and consistency to the elephant's gait. Even though this kind of travel is slow and rocking, I'm still getting somewhere. It is a sensation that is at once soothing and yet forceful."

"See how I don't have to try too hard. The elephant effortlessly carries me (us) on her back."

Silently pondering Kuan Yin's potent communication Lena stops speaking for a moment.

"There is something Kuan Yin is trying to show to me about love, compassion and power," comments Lena, from the depths of her trance. "That just experiencing the power of the elephant moving along is important. Kuan Yin is also telling me to listen to the sounds of the jungle, to just be with what is.

'But Kuan Yin,' I now ask. 'How do I know when to push or to just sit and be with something?'

I'm going to be silent for a moment and listen to Kuan Yin's answer. I'm getting the impression that Kuan Yin is trying to show me how to be aware of the signals. When I said to you, Hope, I was going to listen for Kuan Yin's answer, I noticed that the elephant turned and went towards a small lake."

"The elephant needs a drink of water," Kuan Yin explains in a matter-of-fact way. "So she temporarily veers off the path, traveling to the lake. When she's satisfied she'll return to the original path. The elephant's 'break' then, is good for everyone involved, helping them to get along better."

"We've now returned to the trail. Kuan Yin knows where we're heading. She has a stick in her hand."

"It's a *directional* tool. I would never hurt anything. Instead, I just touch one or the other flank, to instruct the elephant which way I want to go. One can't just 'hit life' and expect it will co-operate, go the way one wants. Maybe it will and maybe it won't. You might have heard the sayings, 'the path is the goal' or 'the journey is the goal'. These sayings are often antithetical to the reality of living in your culture. Your culture is very "goal structured". There is frequently a push to be "where one is supposed to be" rather than savoring where one is right now," observes Kuan Yin.

This is cultural, not instinctual. Naturally, one needs a driving force to survive. However, the concept of having specific goals is very Western. This kind of mindset makes people very ambitious. However, no one is obligated to live his life by this Western view of things.

It is important to have an idea of the path one wants to be on. This statement comes with the warning that one not be too attached to the outcome. To have a concept about the nature of one's life path can be a skillful tool in living one's life. However, there is a danger that one will misconstrue a goal to be the entire purpose of one's life and in so doing perhaps create a negative driving force. Don't be too harsh on yourself concerning the choices you've made during your life. When one subtracts from the equation of life physical birth and death, one can regard lessons learned as forming an infinite line.

Then one can say, 'I'm learning this right now'. Try to crystallize the components of the lesson, excluding as much as is possible gender and financial factors. Repeat to yourself: 'this is the lesson I'm learning right now, at this exact moment in time'.

Lena, you're not always going to feel as though your life is so stagnant. In a year or so, things could dramatically change. Refuse to accept the belief that you don't have options. Right now it may seem that way. Down the road, however, there will be changes, more opportunities. Don't lose sight of the vision you have for you and your family."

"Sometimes, I don't know how much to ask for from others," responds Lena. "I don't know how much I deserve. Do I just ask? Should I ask for more love? Should I expect more from my life? Kuan Yin is telling me there is no easy answer to my questions. However, she says the answer does involve the quality of communication between partners and/or friends."

"What makes any kind of relationship begin and then work is an initial communication," continues Kuan Yin. "Following the initial communication there is always an adjustment. For example, someone has a question. Whatever information is exchanged impacts both the person who has presented the question and the person who responds. Information has been shared and everyone involved makes some kind of an adjustment. There are constant adjustments resulting from communication.

It is similar to other balancing processes that can occur in life. Perhaps no where as much as in relationships does the vibrational nature of thoughts and words become apparent. It's a matter of adjusting how hard one pushes. Patience," Kuan Yin urges. "One needs to always be attentive. Things will go more smoothly in a relationship when avoiding two frequent mistakes:

The first is when there is little or no communication between people. How can adjustments be made if there is no attempt to talk with one another? The second mistake occurs when new information is communicated and the listener refuses to make any adjustment; refuses to *take in and process* any new information.

Let us return, once again, to the elephant. The elephant is a metaphor for the original vehicle; the *driving force* for one's life path. *It* decides and then you decide."

"The elephant's behavior is suddenly becoming very erratic," Lena exclaims, somewhat nervously. "I can't control her direction. She's going every which way."

"Riding upon a female elephant in heat is not so good," acknowledges Kuan Yin. "We can no longer make her our ride down the path. It's not fair to the elephant. We're going to have to trade her in for another elephant or walk."

"We've jumped off the elephant and now we're walking," Lena conveys.

"If you don't have transportation and you want to stay on the path, you'll just have to walk," advises Kuan Yin.

"When one feels pulled to do a particular thing, when one has passion for a certain life path, karma is always involved. In such an instance, (if the goal is worthy and makes one happy), one should continue on that same life path.

Just because the elephant cannot carry you anymore does not mean you should give up your goal. Continue down the path that makes you feel fulfilled. Those who continue on an unrewarding path for the sake of only monetary gain are displaying a lack of trust in life. Continuing in such a mistrustful way could bring impoverishment. Following one's heart, continuing on one's divine path can bring abundance.

One can, however, learn from a partner or friend's poor choices," continues Kuan Yin. "The priority should be to always keep communications open. Formulate and ask good questions. Create a regular time and place for conversations. Regard communications as an ongoing and constructive process," instructs Kuan Yin.

"I realize that in the past, I haven't wanted to make time for communication," Lena confesses. "I guess I'm afraid to ask questions because I'm afraid of heartache and rejection. I'm afraid of hearing what I don't want to hear. Having such constant dread, I rationalize to myself that having no answer is better than having a disappointing answer."

"Anything that helps with growth is positive. Think of positive and original ways of asking questions," encourages Kuan Yin. "When one communicates with love and without expectation, it helps others take a step forward. Open communication discourages relationship stagnation and the creation of stories that may or may not be true."

"Now, we're walking back to the little waterfall (where I usually meet with Kuan Yin). However, I'm seeing it and the bamboo forest from a completely different angle—a different point of view."

Lena pauses for a moment; apparently transfixed upon how one's perspective can drastically change, when observing the same object from a different angle. It seems a perfect opportunity to discuss my newly acquired perspective on the holidays:

***

"As it is the Christmas season, I want to thank you, Kuan Yin, for your insights", I interject softly. "Last week I experienced the return of an old and familiar sadness. I had wished the holidays held more meaning for me and were not so seemingly centered on materialism. I was especially sad about current world events: how my country was still at war and so many souls around the globe are hungry and in need. Sensing your presence that forlorn evening, I heard you say:

'Think of each light and ornament on the Christmas Tree as symbols for loving, compassionate and courageous deeds always occurring somewhere in the world. Brave and charitable acts happen all the time. Make a point of focusing on good deeds. You just need to see and acknowledge them."

(I immediately thought of how my hometown had just completed a modern new shelter for homeless families living in our area.)

"Hope, you say you are frustrated and discouraged about world events. And yet there are extraordinary examples of giving and selflessness in the world. Focus upon positive events, the love and courage of ordinary citizens. There are so many examples demonstrating the strength of the human spirit. I assure you that around the world; important deeds requiring great-heartedness constantly occur. In this season of darkness, let the twinkling ornaments lighten and light up your heart and spirit. In this way, you lend your support and energy to the kind of positive thinking and action that could change the world."

Beginning to speak once again, Lena concludes the reading for today:

"I'm hearing Kuan Yin say she knows I like to laugh. She's very proud that she was able to surprise me and make me laugh at the beginning of the chapter."

"I want to go on meeting with you. I am here to help," re-emphasizes Kuan Yin.

"Kuan Yin is back in a meditative pose, now. She's handing each of us a pomegranate as a parting gift." (A symbol of fertility and abundance, the pomegranate has been regarded as having mysterious healing powers and spiritual significance since ancient times. Therefore, Kuan Yin's gift has special relevance for the above passages.)

Commentary: Emotions and Kuan Yin's Law of Compassion

Beyond her shape-shifts are the goddess's profound parables such as the one above demonstrating her teachings on the creation of abundance. Your beliefs and how you regard yourself make up the living root creating your present pathway. As there is an inbuilt power sharing dynamic, ego's marriage to the emotions is a complicated formula indeed. The ego can feel 'dragged around' by what it regards as superfluous and unnecessary emotionalism. This natural 'joined at the hip' relationship between beliefs and emotions may cause ego to reject and even blame emotions as being subversive to ego's 'progress'.

Stating "It decides and then you decide", Kuan Yin declares that it is the deep emotional impulses welling up from ones very Core that form the guiding, indeed, *driving* forces for any life pathway, setting a given thought-pattern in motion. Your deeply felt love and joy, then, are perfect indicators that you're already traveling your unique path of liberation.

Indeed, one might direct the dream of self-love onto others. Idolatry is the powerful force of love and admiration often projected outward upon celebrities, politicians or other revered personalities. However, this process can be 'hit and miss.' Those who are idolized may, just as easily as they gained your love and admiration, quickly fall from their pedestals. This is because Kuan Yin's Law of Compassion demands that only to the degree that you love yourself can you love others.

Heavily invested in any aspect of fear can cause a state of misalignment with your naturally blissful Authentic Self; resulting in potentially disruptive swings between superiority and inferiority. Emotions could violently catapult from a kind of false ecstasy to abject depression and unworthiness.

On the other hand, alignment of your Immediate and Authentic Self may evoke feelings of joy, love, compassion and fulfillment. These beneficial emotions will, when sustained long term, provide essential support for the mind, body and spirit trinity.

27
Many Flavors of Ice Cream

December 30, 2004: "Each of you has the potential for the God Force potency. However, no individual can *overcome* the God Force. There is a misinterpretation (by some) that Satan is as powerful as God. Limited energy cannot exist on its own. Every experience must exist and yet they (the limiting forces) can never exist on their own. Limited energy, then, is the experience of the *absence* of the God Force (as a teacher and as a belief). Therefore, there is no need to fear it. Those choosing such experiences have a need to understand how it feels to believe evil powers exist. Again, I say that those who pursue this route are taking it too personally. They believe the story they made up about themselves."
-*Kuan Yin*

On Christmas day, the catastrophic Indian Ocean Tsunami made landfall. Claiming hundreds of thousands of lives and displacing millions more, the earthquake (and its resulting wave train) had (in a matter of minutes) wrecked havoc on eleven countries.

Profoundly affected by the news of the suffering millions, Lena also had another, more personal, reason for her grief. Unsuccessful in her efforts to contact close friends living in southern India, she had cried incessantly throughout the days following the event.

Awakened from her dreams, Lena then felt a heavy weight bearing down upon her chest. Aware (from past psychic experiences) that the heaviness was caused by one or more "visiting" energies (souls), she was utterly immobilized, unable to move even her limbs.

Hearing an eerie sound—similar to wind rushing past the side of her face, Lena's efforts to console or dismiss the apparently angry and confused, disembodied spirits seemed futile. Finally they left, freeing her to go back to sleep.

Arriving for her hypnosis appointment a few days later, Lena described this upsetting episode along with a more recent and happier reunion:

"Kuan Yin came very early this morning while I was still asleep," Lena explains, lying back and readying herself to be hypnotized. "She was standing straight up, flying into the room upon something. I couldn't tell exactly what. Nor did I completely understand her purpose for coming. Still, I felt a sense of comfort just having her around."

Upon being counted down Lena immediately found Kuan Yin, and then described her fascinating surroundings:

"We're in the Milky Way; just as in an earlier chapter. Kuan Yin is holding a little box, a treasure chest with light glowing from it. It reminds me of something from a movie. I know she wants to comfort me in my sorrow. I've been asking her for symbols, signs showing what the future holds for me. I want to know so that I can prepare myself. So, I'm just going to look inside the box, now."

There is a short interval and then Lena continues to speak:

"I'm definitely in another country, somewhere in Asia. I can describe it; however I don't know the exact location or name. I see jutting mountains: rocky, pointed peaks with deep canyons in between. It feels very hot and humid and I know that it is my destiny to someday travel here."

"People often say being born in America is lucky," comments Kuan Yin. "It's not necessarily that lucky. Living in the United States can smother one in materialism. Places, like the one in the Eastern hemisphere that you are being shown, Lena, exude a natural and intense spirituality, bringing one closer to a simpler kind of life. While remnants of Western culture could still seep in, these places remain largely unchanged from their ancient traditions. I'd like you to experience (indeed, physically visit) this place; as it will make you more whole, able to help others. Don't resist any opportunities that come along even if something doesn't at the time seem like the right opportunity."

"I'm seeing that my children, too, will travel here with me," affirms Lena. "I'm close to some very ancient structures. I see what I believe is a stone temple. Inside of it now, I feel very cool, almost cold. However, it's the kind of cold that is refreshing. I see also that I will meet some very kind and generous people, people from this remarkable part of the world.

I feel very strongly that I'm meant to go to this place, because in a very real sense, I'm already there. It's very peaceful. When I'm here, there is nothing else that I need. Everything here is made of stone. I'm reclining on a little stone patio, peering out at the beautiful mountains in the distance. The patio sits high above a cavern, allowing me to see from a powerful perspective the vista of the surrounding mountains. I know Kuan Yin wants me to fully experience the peace of this place.

For some reason Hope, I'm seeing your painting of Kuan Yin as an integral part of this vista. I'm going to wait for a moment because Kuan Yin is busy doing some things. She's doing some healing work on someone. I'm just going to sit with her, for a while, and watch what she is doing. She's working on someone who doesn't believe in healing. I warn her, saying, 'He doesn't believe in you!'"

"It doesn't matter," Kuan Yin replies. "Things work even if he doesn't believe in me."

"I'm feeling so overwhelmed by the Tsunami," Lena suddenly remarks. "My husband and I are donating money to various charities. However, I feel our contribution is so miniscule in comparison to the enormous relief effort, the enormous need."

"Again, let me explain," responds Kuan Yin. "I am not being heartless when I say there was nothing anyone could have done beforehand to prevent the earthquake. All anyone has the power to do," continues Kuan Yin, "is develop their faith and trust. It is all anyone can do to understand the *grand plan*. There is life and there is karma. There are so many levels of existence. Different people live on different levels. Everything is very individualized. Those who do not believe may deny all of this because it's too complicated."

"I am recalling a woman who experienced a miracle [during the Tsunami]. She and her home were untouched by the rushing waters," describes Lena, from her trance. "Upon being interviewed by the particular newspaper reporter, she mentioned how she could only watch helplessly as hundreds of victims and dwellings were swiftly washed out to sea. I've heard of other miracles, as well. There are stories of individuals who were tossed about by the raging torrents, only to escape any serious harm."

"That woman's experience is a good example of how everyone lives at *different levels*," notes Kuan Yin. "Imagine if you were living in an era without television and radio. It's very probable that you wouldn't have even heard about this event. Indeed your life, Lena, would be quite different, unaffected by tragedies occurring half way around the world.

I'm trying to demonstrate the importance of positive focus as it pertains to imagining the most expansive possibilities. As I've said before, no one is obligated to fill their mind with negative information. The ego's task is to decide what is relevant for achieving personal fulfillment. Instead of being distracted by constant internal or external 'updates', you have complete freedom to maintain your focused intent upon only those people and events you wish to attract into your life. Learn from the Elders, those Guides who came before me. Come to know the basic universal principles. Be open to new learning opportunities."

Following this profound statement by Kuan Yin, the discussion temporarily lapses.

Then I ask: "Hearing of such natural catastrophes, what is the most helpful thing we can do for the earth and her people, Kuan Yin?"

"Kuan Yin is changing shape in response to your question, Hope. I'm not sure what this particular shape-shifting means, if it is an answer in itself or if she is adjusting to the question" Lena contemplates. "I'll just watch for a moment and try to understand."

"Loving people is the most helpful thing anyone can do," Kuan Yin answers after a short while. "Your society has the resources, at this very moment, to fashion industries and lifestyles conducive to a non-harmful environment. There is a popular belief that over-population is the threat to the earth's environment. However, for many places upon the earth it is also very much a question of resource availability and distribution. There is a real need for creating a holistic infrastructure that can support everyone.

A helpful mindset is *simple-living and high-thinking*", continues Kuan Yin. "Science is constantly evolving. There are now recyclable batteries, ink cartridges, etc. Keep up to date on the latest technologies. Be aware, set examples and create trends that will positively influence people's lives and the environment. As I said earlier, however, this is also a discussion about love and developing a greater capacity to love. It can help everyone.

We're all one huge family, a great continuum. Don't underestimate the power of the love created in your homes and families. This love has an immense potency, the power to influence other's lives in a positive way."

"My other question is about theories concerning 'future lives'," I continue, addressing Kuan Yin while Lena takes a momentary break. "Rather than allowing fear to take hold, when contemplating the inevitability of death, I'm sometimes able to regard it as a new opportunity, the prospect for a new life.

"I'm seeing a beautiful beam of light," responds Lena almost instantaneously. "It represents the oneness of human consciousness."

"You've already lived any *future lives*, *all* of your lives!" Kuan Yin states emphatically. "There is no such thing as time! I want the theme of this final chapter to be that humans need not take everything that happens to them and around them so seriously. Such an approach to living can create pain.

Some people believe that death is a punishment from God rather than a natural progression, a doorway to other realities. By having such a grim perspective, they make it a fearful and painful experience. I repeat! Just don't take everything so personally. In fact, if humans didn't cling to events in their lives, every experience that ever was could be lived in an instant. However, it is often the nature of ego to want to possess things.

And sometimes, it doesn't want to let go. The ego's fear of letting go can be compared to a fear of falling."

"I comprehend how simplicity facilitates a certain ease in one's life," states Lena.

"So much of what humans do in their lives is based upon grabbing", reasserts Kuan Yin. "Ego usually wants to grab, hold onto situations. Even the physical items people collect are connected to the emotions they are stuck in. One can find clues to a person's emotions by observing his/her possessions. Humans are absorbed in 'tasting' everything that shows up during the *journey*. However, one cannot taste *everything* without eventually getting a bellyache!

Compared to the other spiritual realms, human senses are quite limited. In these other realms there are more senses, more enjoyment. However, even in these other realms the ego wants to hold onto things, situations. Our spirit knows we don't die nor are we born. If our ego knew what our greater self knows, it would not fear disaster. Caught up in a new incarnation, one may forget their Always State, Form; perhaps forgetting everything from before. However, one is *already always that!* There is only eternity, knowledge and bliss. But one could still be terrified that it might not be true. That is ego at work. Ego can keep one from being free.

Lena wants to taste all these experiences. And the ego makes it possible. Don't curse the ego. So many scriptures curse the ego self. Instead, regard your life as about choices, experiences and desire and that you are already liberated. Don't be afraid of desire. It is why you're here: to taste, *live*."

"That sounds sinful," responds Lena. "Certain friends of mine wouldn't necessarily agree with your philosophy about life, Kuan Yin."

"If they don't want to play, then go somewhere else. They want to believe what they want to believe. Just move on. See? Don't take everything so personally. It's just an 'agreement' you all made when you took on an ego. You splintered off from the whole."

"I'd like to know more about this "agreement"," I interject.

"Kuan Yin is showing me visually how I'm (we all are) part of a round ball of light that people call God," delineates Lena.

"There are those who would rather God were thought of as a person, a man with a white beard," elaborates Kuan Yin. "However, for purposes of this manuscript, I will continue with this ball of light analogy of the God Force. Those who object to my use of the word 'God' or 'God Force' will just have to deal with it for now."

"I'm seeing not pie-shaped but straight slivers coming from this central ball of light," depicts Lena. "These straight slivers of light become a person who plays out adventures from his or her beliefs. When you put all the slivers together they form God. It is as if one takes a small chip of gold from a cave made of gold. The cave and chip of gold are separate. Yet, they are the same. How can this be?"

Answering her own question, Lena comments, "Because they are both comprised of the same chemical elements. Why do we even go through such a complex process? Is it all just a beautiful game?" Lena asks Kuan Yin.

"The God Force likes intense pleasure," expounds Kuan Yin. "However, the God Force experiences itself more clearly when it can separate itself out; obtaining a different point of view. Because of this separation, the personification of the "Always Self", there is the possibility for pain.

"Experiential versus the God eye! Possessing 'ego vision', a person's view through her/his physical eyes is quite versatile, able to discern wide and varied vistas over huge distances and/or scrutinizing the minutest of details.

Ego's very nature: capable of relatively expansive, detailed, and yet *individualistic* perspective is crucial. Separating itself out from the God Force, ego extracts infinite unique experiences, integral to humanity's process of *spiritualizing matter*. Incarnating on the earth, achieving individualism is therefore critical for attainment of divinity.

Individualism may cause momentary estrangement from the God Self. However, this person has forgotten that they are *everything* in the mirror, the sliver *and* the ball of light," continues Kuan Yin.

During this complex passage Lena was inundated by infinite rapid-fire visuals: emanations from the God Mind.

"Further and unfortunately, wrong assumptions are made about suffering. Some individuals even believe that it is *required*, that suffering brings one closer to salvation. Quite the contrary," disputes Kuan Yin, "the God Force likes to play. Therefore, if all individuals could unite creating a real sense of community many problems could be healed.

The God Force is separate and not separate, whole and not whole at the same time. Really, it is not 'sliceable', not reducible. Even when it is sliced into individual energies, it does not diminish the total God Force *or* the power of the individual.

Each of you has the potential for the God Force potency. However, no individual can *overcome* the God Force. There is a misinterpretation, (by some) that Satan is as powerful as God. Limited energy cannot live on its own. Every experience must exist and yet they (the limiting forces) can never exist on their own. Limited energy, then, is the experience of the *absence* of the God Force. Therefore, there is no need to fear it.

Those choosing such experiences have a need to understand how it feels to believe evil powers exist. Again, I say those who pursue this route are taking it too personally. They believe the story they've made up about themselves.

It is similar to a person going into an ice cream store and only choosing one flavor from many. Preoccupied with tasting that flavor for a very long time, they are probably quite sick and tired of it. Still, they don't want to believe there are any other flavors available. The "agreement", then, is to continue to *believe* in that particular flavor. Here's where reincarnation and its opportunity for experiencing a vast array of perspectives, "agreements", enters in. Another life offers another opportunity, a chance to 'switch flavors' so to speak.

Taking oneself too personally, however, can cause a soul to get caught up, stuck in redundancy: in a particular (and perhaps unfortunate) *flavor*. In such instances, the individual is forgetting one has the ability to *choose* his or her flavors, *lives*," contends Kuan Yin.

"As I near the end of this passage and the manuscript I repeat: 'don't take things too personally'. I have demonstrated the pitfalls of taking life too personally in the negative sense: to *identify* too much with a limiting "flavor" (belief). However, I want my readers to also be wary of taking even life's *positive* accomplishments or identities too seriously, as well," Kuan Yin cautions.

"When identifying too strongly with a particular achievement or persona, people can automatically loop into repetitive and entrapping lifetimes. Clinging to *any* former identity (expansive or limiting), then, may act as a roadblock, preventing one from experiencing other flavors."

Commentary: Attract Only Those 'Flavors' You Wish for Your Life

Riveted by Kuan Yin's assertion of *"the great mix of karma (made-up stories) and free will"*, I understood that even a moment spent on regret or sorrow is one less moment joyously attracting. Still, becoming "quite sick and tired of a particular (limiting) *flavor*" i.e. chronic self-pity or fear, could evolve into an important learning opportunity; a chance to transform any limiting vibrations.

We are not meant to suffer, nor are we destined to endure endless entrapping, "made-up" realities. Rather, releasing whatever obstructive beliefs one might possess could open the way to the realization that personal attention and intention are running the entire show. Therefore, focus on the expansive possibilities within yourself.

An elevated form of appreciation, marveling allows us to continue the process by internalizing those beneficial elements surrounding us.

There are those sometimes unyielding beliefs, however, that can, at least temporarily, undermine one's free will to focus upon one's dreams. If one has become too diminished in their perspective; he or she may feel a need to compensate by embracing a narrow reality framework. One might, for example, believe in an overly-romanticized justification for suffering: that suffering somehow "brings one nearer to salvation". Or, that suffering somehow validates one's existence. Combined with the "not enough", "better than" or "survival of the fittest" belief, this mindset can balloon into a storm of confusion, causing one to make life-sabotaging decisions.

However, we are in no way obligated to assume the "artificial burden" of idealized struggle and suffering. Kuan Yin has stated that we each are living our own unique vision of a "realistic life" and also have the ability to change it. The earth is a place where "smaller energies" can evolve into "larger, stronger energies". Kuan Yin states that the very act of choosing to be born on the earth means we are learning to "think ourselves there"; that we have the potential to align ourselves with our highest vibration. By highlighting the numerous positive events of your life, you can heal any erroneous mindsets, successfully "thinking yourself" to a place of peace and abundance.

28
Eight Senses

March 16, 2005: "Practicing this deceptively easy meditation helps each of us to *see* reality. When Kuan Yin refers to *reality*, she really means truth, the importance of life.
Some may need to practice distancing themselves from materialism while others may need to get more grounded in the material world. This meditation can, when properly implemented, balance these two types of people."
-*Lena Lees*

Several weeks before Lena and I met again, I experienced an interesting, lucid dream. In my waking reality, I live near a large open space, a large green dotted with oaks and redwoods. This is relevant as this very field was the setting:

In the dream, a cow was apparently lost, roaming about in a field that was across the street from my house. Eventually it began to slowly approach. Looking out my window, I realized the cow was determined to charge my front door. Hiding, frightened, I watched from behind a drapery as the animal stormed the house.

Once inside, milling about, she wasn't destructive in any way. Curious, meandering through the house for a short while, the cow quite suddenly departed. Finally having the courage to look around, I realized that the furnishings were completely untouched. It was as if she'd never been there. Had I not seen the cow trotting about, through my own eyes, I would have never believed something so extraordinary had occurred.

Going out for errands, later and then returning home, I looked around to see if the cow was still in the general outside area. Determining she was nowhere in sight, I was curious enough to further explore the field.

Mysteriously drawn to a daisy-blanketed knoll, I discovered a newborn calf curled up, resting peacefully beneath the wide-canopy oak tree. I intuitively knew the sweet tan and white calf was the heifer's offspring, her gift to the world.

I think earlier that same night or on a previous night, I dreamt of a two headed cow, just watching as I passed by. I couldn't help but wonder whether its two heads represented human consciousness's ability to scan the mind's inward and outward manifestations.

Analyzing the dream, mindful of the imminent completion of the manuscript, I was certain the calf was one of Kuan Yin's polymorphisms. I believe, now, this was her way of explaining that with the completion of chapter twenty-eight Lena and I had come full circle, that this segment would signal the finale; at least for now.

***

Joining me for an evening session, Lena explains how things have been so cerebral for her lately (with family, work and school), that she doesn't recall any unusual Kuan Yin experiences. Then, retracing her thoughts, she suddenly mentions observing something curious just a few days earlier:

Having viewed the vacation photos taken when her husband and son visited Hawaii, she couldn't help but notice something peculiar. Whoever had taken the snapshots had (intentionally or unintentionally) included in the background of almost all of the images, various garden, pool and fountain statues of Kuan Yin.

Now, counting Lena down to her trance state, I became aware that she had found herself on some Kuan Yin island. One, she admits from within her trance, she knows little about:

"I see the temple and a large statue of Kuan Yin up on the hill. The ocean is nearby. I see the caves and passages inland, where monks once must have lived. I believe this island is the one across the waterway from Shanghai."

"The island of Pu Tuo Shan?"

"Yes, I'm almost certain that's where I am right now. I remember visiting here before in a previous trance. Kuan Yin feels very dedicated to these villagers. Here, there is such a strong sense of tradition, supportive energy for the simple folk, the fishermen and women.

I'm just going to see what Kuan Yin has to say. I just want to see if she has a specific message and/or a specific audience, even if it is just for one person. I'll just wait for her response."

"Sit with me in divine faith and believe in me. And I'll be there. This goes for all beings," greets Kuan Yin.

"I'm feeling Kuan Yin has an important message but I don't know how to articulate it. It's something very powerful but simple. I just need to sit with Kuan Yin to understand."

There ensues a long silence as Lena attempts to decipher the information being presented by Kuan Yin:

"It's an interesting dichotomy", continues Lena; "trying to grapple with one's dilemma about being in the material world. Kuan Yin is telling me that instead of seeing things and events separately, we should perceive them as part of the whole. Conversely, she is saying we also forget to notice the little things, a single stone or grain of sand. So, the existential question is: when to notice the little things and when to see things as a whole.

A powerful meditation when contemplating the Oneness of everything is to find something's unique qualities. For instance, observe an island's wholeness and then the uniqueness of a single stone. Westerners are dealing with this dichotomy on a grand scale. Kuan Yin wants me to emphasize that Her meditation is simple but powerful. It's like physical exercise. One can practice it just once a day or as often as one likes.

Other examples to meditate upon besides an island and an individual stone on the island beach are faces in a crowd or a leaf on a tree. Each person in the crowd is, naturally, unique and yet, at that same moment, part of the whole. The same is true for leaves on the trees. Practicing this deceptively easy meditation helps each of us to *see* reality.

When Kuan Yin refers to *reality*, she really means truth, the importance of life. Some may need to practice distancing themselves from materialism while others may need to become more grounded in the material world. This meditation can, when properly implemented, balance these two types of people.

Wow! Suddenly, I'm feeling Kuan Yin's energy tonight. She is emanating powerful love and peace. She's smiling with great approval," Lena relays.

"Lena, you think you're supposed to be doing something else, but in your life you're doing what you're supposed to. You're on the right path. I'm very pleased with the cover art for the book. I'll continue sending Hope important dreams. I have a very personal relationship with her."

Just then Lena said, "You know, Hope, how it is quite difficult for me to channel Kuan Yin without you being present?"

"Yes, we seem to work well together."

"I don't quite understand," ponders Lena. "Oh I'm seeing how it all works, now. It's alchemy! It's like two wires coming together to create a spark. It's similar to intimate relationships. Kuan Yin is happy with her connection with you Hope. I'm seeing a graphic. It's as if Kuan Yin sends you a band of energy. The band looks almost like the Milky Way, where nebulas are constantly born."

Suddenly commenting, Kuan Yin says: "I want to send a simple message, something everyone can participate in and that won't complicate their lives. This book is the best starting point for the era we're living in. It's a thread—a rope to a life-saving raft. The meditation I've included is quite appropriate for the ending of the book. And as it is right in this chapter, my readers will be left contemplating this one simple practice as they close the book. After all, each individual has a busy life. Not everyone can be a monk, devoted only to spiritual practices."

The topic of earth's karmic oil cycle (previously discussed in chapter fourteen) quite suddenly resurfaces in the conversation. (Indeed, the tragic 2010 Gulf of Mexico Oil Spill illustrates the stark need for a more comprehensive understanding of our absolute environmental and economic dependence upon a healthy ecosphere.)

"As I have mentioned, oil drilling and its relationship to the 'better than' and 'not enough' beliefs being played out on earth reaches far forward and back in history," informs Kuan Yin. "The entire topic is more about an energy manifested from planetary beliefs, rather than specific people. It's just that certain souls volunteered to be a part of this drama. It's going to take thirty or forty years to break out of the oil cycle."

Quite disappointed, Lena laments, "I'd hoped it might be less."
Joining in, I exclaim, "I had too."
"Not so! It will take quite a bit longer than you had anticipated, my dear ones," insists Kuan Yin gently. "There is free will, but this [cycle] has to run its course. There's just a cycle which must be completed."

"Yeah," comments Lena. "I'm seeing a bunch of sticky, gooey stuff in the future. Now, I'm asking Kuan Yin if there's anything further you, Hope, can do to keep yourself healthy and energetic."

"She's telling me you need to spiritually 'clear' every corner of your house. She says every corner but one has clear energy. I'm seeing and feeling that right now. Wow, I guess Feng Shui really does work.

She's also telling me that in the future, you will have a close relationship with your grandson, Hope; that it is karmic. One of the main reasons he came to earth was to meet you."

I then asked Kuan Yin if she believed there would be another Kuan Yin book.

"If another book *created itself*, it will emerge from how the original book is received," advises Kuan Yin. "There is an evolution involved in all of this, which is intimately connected with what is sometimes referred to as *the power of the word*. I need to clarify something here," Kuan Yin continues. "When I say 'power of the word', I am speaking in general and not religious terms.

Right now, the book is in an electronic format. Not finished, it is still being composed and edited. It will probably take longer before it is actually in physical print. Because of free will, the reactions of *all* beings as well as reactions emanating from all events, I want to wait to respond to your question. I want to analyze the response and the final outcome. I'm not just speaking of individual reactions. There is an *energetic reaction* to something in print. That is what is really meant by the power of the word. There is a reaction even from the universe to the energetic quality of a book.

Writers know this. So do Hope and her husband, John, who is helping edit the book. From such reactions, another and another energy is created. The 'power of the word', then, cannot be triggered until the book is actually in print. I want to also emphasize that you are in the *printed word* of your humanity.

"You know, Hope, how Kuan Yin usually leaves us with a parting gift?"

"Yes."

"Well, she's given us something as a parting gift but I can't tell what it is. So I'm going to ask her.

'What is it Kuan Yin?'

"It's right there!"

"Where?" inquires Lena, "I think I will probably need at least twenty senses to figure out what this is."

"Someone with eight senses would understand. I can see what I gave you both. However, not perceiving it doesn't mean it is less effective."

Commentary: The Wondrous Opportunity

Kuan Yin wants us to know that we have great freedom while living on earth. Contrary to the belief that evil lurks just around the corner, She asserts that any such concept is born of dualism. Only when we become trapped in limiting "agreements"; taking things too personally, do we repress our natural ability to beneficially choose. Releasing any false and imprisoning concepts, we unlock our full power to attract our most expansive reality:

"Kuan Yin is morphing again, doing incredible things to show how life isn't stagnant. Our experiences are ever changing, flowing. She's forming something and then something else."

The Deity maintains that reincarnation is our opportunity for experiencing a vast array of perspectives; *flavors*. Another life offers another opportunity, a chance to "switch flavors". Beyond intriguing and beautiful, her bountiful transformations help illustrate the possibilities and pitfalls of our own creative nature. Whether playful or ominous: her morphing alludes to our own multidimensionality; how we have already lived *all of our lives*.

Kuan Yin's shape shifts demonstrate how we are divine and powerful "slices" of the God Force. When *playing out* lifetimes (our prismatic incarnations), we are to remain aware of the presence of the "Always Self"; that which is eternal. Kuan Yin's myriad forms demonstrate the boundlessness of free will: that innate force which can ultimately lead us back to all-encompassing compassion and oneness.

The everyday events of our lives offer wondrous opportunities to attune our deeply resonant "tissues of the soul" to the natural world and vice versa. This is the miracle of Kuan Yin's Law of Compassion. Ironically, it is the three limiting beliefs, when skillfully processed and reconciled; that could stimulate that intimately cathartic evolution; drawing one ever closer to their fully realized humanity. Focused beneficial intention and attention are the "driving forces"; allowing us to effectively direct, attract and transform energy from infinite combinations so to crystallize an expansive personal goal.

To deeply assess personal and mass dramas, skillfully interacting with them can assist one's spiritual growth. Kuan Yin advises that even in circumstances where events appear to be so unfair, individuals will especially need to summon compassion, patience and resilience to cope.

There is a way to regard even supposed setbacks as *opportunities* for personal and/or mass growth. Utilizing Kuan Yin's focused intent; one could discover any potential positive advantage. At the mass level, interest groups with common goals can prioritize helpful beliefs and practical solutions.

Such deep introspection concerning any unfortunate event has the potential to trigger crucial life changes: *"With practice, a reality is created somewhere having the very consciousness of loving kindness. Such practice also draws one to those loving kindness planes of consciousness."* These can then lead to new personal/mass understanding and reprioritizing: a *shifting* of both kinds of Evolutionary Potentials. Even if we can only partially resolve these episodes, we have nevertheless succeeded in becoming more self-aware.

ABOUT THE AUTHOR

Bringing to *Oracle of Compassion: The Living Word of Kuan Yin* her extensive studies in ancient and contemporary wisdom and philosophy, Ms Bradford has acquired more then a quarter of a century expertise in Transpersonal Hypnosis. In spite of her professional credentials and experience, she could never have imagined the singular psychic event that would transform her life. Commencing in the winter of 2004 a hypnosis client, Lena Lees spontaneously channeled Eastern deity of compassion Kuan Yin. She revealed Her immutable teachings on the Law of Compassion. As witness and transcriber, Ms. Bradford now offers the amended version of these channelings (with commentaries): bringing to you Kuan Yin's world-renowned compassion and spiritual teachings. Ms. Bradford's theoretical discussion on the deity's esoteric teachings (and their relationship to everyday life situations) offers an in-depth evaluation of these spiritual principles. Ms. Bradford is also the author of *Beneficial Law of Attraction: the Manifestation Teachings*.

Made in the USA
Lexington, KY
14 March 2019